BENCHMARK SERIES

Microsoft® Word 2016

Level 1

Workbook

Rutkosky • Roggenkamp • Rutkosky

St. Paul

Senior Vice President	Linda Hein
Editor in Chief	Christine Hurney
Director of Production	Timothy W. Larson
Production Editor	Jen Weaverling
Cover and Text Designer	Valerie King
Copy Editors	Communicáto, Ltd.
Senior Design and Production Specialist	Jack Ross
Assistant Developmental Editors	Mamie Clark, Katie Werdick
Testers	Janet Blum, Fanshawe College; Traci Post
Instructional Support Writers	Janet Blum, Fanshawe College; Brienna McWade
Indexer	Terry Casey
Vice President Information Technology	Chuck Bratton
Digital Projects Manager	Tom Modl
Vice President Sales and Marketing	Scott Burns
Director of Marketing	Lara Weber McLellan

Cover Photo Credits: © Photomall/Dreamstime.com

ISBN 978-0-76386-924-3 (digital)
ISBN 978-0-76387-155-0 (print)

875 Montreal Way
St. Paul, MN 55102
Email: educate@emcp.com
Website: ParadigmCollege.com

Printed in the United States of America

24 23 22 21 20 19 18 17 16 3 4 5 6 7 8 9 10 11 12

Contents

WORD 2016

Microsoft®

Word Level 1

Unit 1

Editing and Formatting Documents

Microsoft® Word

Preparing a Word Document

CHAPTER 1

Study Tools

Study tools include a presentation and a list of chapter Quick Steps and Hint margin notes. Use these resources to help you further develop and review skills learned in this chapter.

Concepts Check

Check your understanding by identifying application tools used in this chapter. If you are a SNAP user, launch the Concepts Check from your Assignments page..

Recheck

Check your understanding by taking this quiz. If you are a SNAP user, launch the Recheck from your Assignments page.

Skills Exercise

Additional activities are available to SNAP users. If you are a SNAP user, access these activities from your Assignments page.

Skills Assessment

Assessment 1

Type and Edit a Document on Resume Writing

1. Open Word and then type the text in Figure WB-1.1. Correct any errors highlighted by the spelling checker. Include only one space after end-of-sentence punctuation. Use the New Line command, Shift + Enter, to end the line after *Created by Marie Solberg* and *Monday, October 8, 2018*.
2. Make the following changes to the document:
   a. Delete the first occurrence of the word *currently* in the first sentence of the first paragraph.
   b. Select the word *important* in the first sentence in the first paragraph and then type essential.
   c. Type and hard-hitting between the words *concise* and *written* in the second sentence of the second paragraph.
   d. Delete the words *over and over,* (including the comma) in the third sentence in the second paragraph.
   e. Select and then delete the second sentence of the third paragraph (the sentence that begins *So do not take*).
   f. Join the second and third paragraphs.
   g. Delete the name *Marie Solberg* and then type your first and last names.
3. Save the document and name it **1-WriteResume**.
4. Print and then close **1-WriteResume.docx**.

Figure WB-1.1 Assessment 1

> Writing a Resume
>
> For every job seeker, including those currently employed and those currently not working, a powerful resume is an important component of the job search. In fact, conducting a job search without a resume is virtually impossible. A resume is your calling card that briefly communicates the skills, qualifications, experience, and value you bring to the prospective employer. It is the document that will open doors and generate interviews.
>
> Your resume is a sales document, and you are the product. You must identify the features of that product, and then communicate them in a concise written presentation. Remind yourself over and over, as you work your way through the resume process, that you are writing marketing literature designed to market yourself.
>
> Your resume can have tremendous power and a phenomenal impact on your job search. So do not take it lightly. You should devote the time, energy, and resources that are essential to developing a resume that is well written, visually attractive, and effective in communicating who you are and how you want to be perceived.
>
> Created by Marie Solberg
> Monday, October 8, 2018
> Note: Please insert this information between the 2nd and 3rd sections.

Assessment 2 — Check the Spelling and Grammar of a Resume Style Document

Data Files

1. Open **ResumeStyles.docx**.
2. Save the document with the name **1-ResumeStyles**.
3. Complete a spelling and grammar check on the document and correct the errors.
4. Type the sentence Different approaches work for different people. between the first and second sentences in the first paragraph of text below the title *RESUME STYLES*.
5. Move the insertion point to the end of the document, type your first and last names, press Shift + Enter, and then type the current date.
6. Save, print, and then close **1-ResumeStyles.docx**.

Assessment 3 — Create a Document Describing Keyboard Shortcuts

1. Press F1 to display the Word Help window.
2. Click in the search text box, type keyboard shortcuts, and then press the Enter key.
3. At the Word Help window, click the Keyboard shortcuts for Microsoft Word 2016 for Windows hyperlink.
4. Read through the information in the Word Help window.
5. Open a new blank single-spaced document by clicking the File tab, clicking the *New* option, and then double-clicking the *Single spaced (blank)* template.
6. Create a document with the following specifications:
   a. Type Keyboard Shortcuts as the title.
   b. Describe four keyboard shortcuts with a brief description of how each shortcut is used.
   c. Click in the title *Keyboard Shortcuts* and then use the Tell Me feature to center the title.

7. Save the document and name it **1-KeyboardShortcuts**.
8. Print and then close **1-KeyboardShortcuts.docx**.

Visual Benchmark

Create a Letter

1. At a blank document, type the personal business letter shown in Figure WB-1.2 on the next page following the directions in red.
2. Save the completed letter and name it **1-CoverLtr**.
3. Print and then close the document.

Case Study

Part 1

You are the assistant to Paul Brewster, the training coordinator at a medium-sized service-oriented business. You have been asked by Mr. Brewster to prepare a document for Microsoft Word users within the company explaining the steps employees should take to save an open company contract document to a folder named *Contracts* that is located in the *Documents* main folder. Create the document explaining the steps and then save the document and name it **1-Saving**. Print and then close the document.

Part 2

Mr. Brewster would like to have a document containing a brief summary of some basic Word commands for use in Microsoft Word training classes. He has asked you to prepare a document containing the following information:

- A brief explanation of how to move the insertion point to a specific page
- Keyboard shortcuts to move the insertion point to the beginning and end of a text line and the beginning and end of a document
- Commands to delete text from the insertion point to the beginning of a word and from the insertion point to the end of a word
- Steps to select a word and a paragraph using the mouse
- A keyboard shortcut to select the entire document

Save the completed document and name it **1-WordCommands**. Print and then close the document.

Part 3

According to Mr. Brewster, the company is considering updating the Human Resources Department computers to Microsoft Office 2016. He has asked you to use the Internet to go to the Microsoft home page at www.microsoft.com and then use the Search feature to find information on the system requirements for Office Professional Plus 2016. When you find the information, type a document that contains the Office Professional Plus 2016 system requirements for the computer and processor, memory, hard disk space, and operating system. Save the document and name it **1-SystemReq**. Print and then close the document.

Figure WB-1.2 Visual Benchmark

(press Enter three times)

4520 South Park Street *(press Shift + Enter)*
Newark, NJ 07122 *(press Shift + Enter)*
Current Date *(press Enter two times)*

Mrs. Sylvia Hammond *(press Shift + Enter)*
Sales Director, Eastern Division *(press Shift + Enter)*
Grand Style Products *(press Shift + Enter)*
1205 Sixth Street *(press Shift + Enter)*
Newark, NJ 07102 *(press Enter)*

Dear Mrs. Hammond: *(press Enter)*

Thank you for agreeing to meet with me next Wednesday. Based on our initial conversation, it seems that my ability to sell solutions rather than products is a good fit for your needs as you seek to expand your visibility in the region. *(press Enter)*

As noted in the enclosed resume, I have led an under-performing product division to generating 33 percent of total revenue (up from 5 percent) at our location, and delivering, from a single location, 25 percent of total sales for our 20-site company. Having completed this turnaround over the last 5 years, I'm eager for new challenges where my proven skills in sales, marketing, and program/event planning can contribute to a company's bottom line. *(press Enter)*

I have been thinking about the challenges you described in building your presence at the retail level, and I have some good ideas to share at our meeting. I am excited about the future of Grand Style Products and eager to contribute to your growth. *(press Enter)*

Sincerely, *(press Enter two times)*

Student Name *(press Enter)*

Enclosure

Microsoft® Word

Formatting Characters and Paragraphs

CHAPTER 2

Study Tools

Study tools include a presentation and a list of chapter Quick Steps and Hint margin notes. Use these resources to help you further develop and review skills learned in this chapter.

Concepts Check

Check your understanding by identifying application tools used in this chapter. If you are a SNAP user, launch the Concepts Check from your Assignments page..

Recheck

Check your understanding by taking this quiz. If you are a SNAP user, launch the Recheck from your Assignments page.

Skills Exercise

Additional activities are available to SNAP users. If you are a SNAP user, access these activities from your Assignments page.

Skills Assessment

Assessment 1

Data Files

Apply Character Formatting to a Lease Agreement Document

1. Open **LeaseAgrmnt.docx** and then save it with the name **2-LeaseAgrmnt**.
2. Press Ctrl + End to move the insertion point to the end of the document, press the Enter key, and then type the text shown in Figure WB-2.1. Bold, italicize, and underline text as shown.
3. Select the entire document and then change the font to 12-point Candara.
4. Select and then bold *THIS LEASE AGREEMENT* in the first paragraph.
5. Select and then italicize *12 o'clock midnight* in the *Term* section.
6. Select the title *LEASE AGREEMENT* and then change the font to 16-point Corbel and the font color to standard dark blue. (The title should remain bold.)
7. Select the heading *Term*, change the font to 14-point Corbel, and then apply small caps formatting. (The heading should remain bold.)
8. Use Format Painter to change the formatting to small caps in 14-point Corbel bold for the remaining headings (*Rent*, *Damage Deposit*, *Use of Premises*, *Condition of Premises*, *Alterations and Improvements*, *Damage to Premises*, and *Inspection of Premises*).
9. Save, print, and then close **2-LeaseAgrmnt.docx**.

Figure WB-2.1 Assessment 1

Inspection of Premises

Lessor shall have the right at all reasonable times during the term of this Agreement to exhibit the Premises and to display the usual *for rent* or *vacancy* signs on the Premises at any time within forty-five days before the expiration of this Lease.

Assessment 2

Data Files

Apply Styles, a Style Set, and a Theme to a Hardware Technology Document

1. Open **NetworkHardware.docx** and then save it with the name **2-NetworkHardware**.
2. Apply the Heading 1 style to the title *Network Hardware*.
3. Apply the Heading 2 style to the headings in the document (*Hubs*, *Switches*, *Repeaters*, *Routers*, *Gateways*, *Bridges*, and *Network Interface Cards*).
4. Apply the Lines (Stylish) style set.
5. Apply the Savon theme.
6. Apply the Green theme colors.
7. Apply the Georgia theme fonts.
8. Apply the Open paragraph spacing.
9. Highlight in yellow the second sentence in the *Hubs* section.
10. Save, print, and then close **2-NetworkHardware.docx**.

Assessment 3

Data Files

Apply Character and Paragraph Formatting to an Employee Privacy Document

1. Open **WorkplacePrivacy.docx** and then save it with the name **2-WorkplacePrivacy**.
2. With the insertion point positioned at the beginning of the document (on the blank line), type WORKPLACE PRIVACY.
3. Select the text from the beginning of the first paragraph to the end of the document (being sure to select the blank line at the end of the document) and then make the following changes:
   a. Change the line spacing to 1.5 lines.
   b. Change the spacing after paragraphs to 0 points.
   c. Indent the first line of each paragraph 0.5 inch.
   d. Change the paragraph alignment to justified alignment.
4. Move the insertion point to the end of the document and, if necessary, drag the First Line Indent marker on the horizontal ruler back to 0 inch. Type the text shown in Figure WB-2.2. (Create a hanging indent, as shown in Figure WB-2.2.)
5. Select the entire document and then change the font to Constantia.
6. Select the title *WORKPLACE PRIVACY*, center it, change the font to 14-point Calibri bold, and then apply the Fill - Orange, Accent 2, Outline - Accent 2 text effect (third column, first row in the Text Effects and Typography button drop-down gallery).
7. Use the Format Painter to apply the same formatting to the title *BIBLIOGRAPHY* that you applied to the title *WORKPLACE PRIVACY*.
8. Save, print, and then close **2-WorkplacePrivacy.docx**.

Figure WB-2.2 Assessment 3

BIBLIOGRAPHY

Amaral, H. G. (2018). *Privacy in the workplace,* 2nd edition (pp. 103-112). Denver, CO: Goodwin Publishing Group.

Visual Benchmark

Create an Active Listening Report

1. At a blank document, press the Enter key two times and then type the document shown in Figure WB-2.3. Set the body text in 12-point Cambria, set the title in 16-point Candara bold, set the headings in 14-point Candara bold, change the paragraph spacing after the headings to 6 points, change the font color to standard dark blue for the entire document, and then apply additional formatting so the document appears as shown in the figure.
2. Save the document and name it **2-ActiveListen**.
3. Print and then close the document.

Figure WB-2.3 Visual Benchmark

ACTIVE LISTENING SKILLS

Speaking and listening is a two-way activity. When the audience pays attention, the speaker gains confidence, knowing that his or her message is being received and appreciated. At the same time, alert listeners obtain information, hear an amusing or interesting story, and otherwise benefit from the speaker's presentation.

Become an Active Listener

Active listeners pay attention to the speaker and to what is being said. They are respectful of the speaker and eager to be informed or entertained. In contrast, *passive listeners* "tune out" the presentation and may even display rudeness by not paying attention to the speaker. Here are ways in which you can become an active listener:

Listen with a purpose: Stay focused on what the speaker is saying and you will gain useful information or hear a suspenseful story narrated well. Try to avoid letting your attention wander.

Be courteous: Consider that the speaker spent time preparing for the presentation and thus deserves your respect.

Take brief notes: If the speaker is providing information, take brief notes on the main ideas. Doing so will help you understand and remember what is being said. If you have questions or would like to hear more about a particular point, ask the speaker for clarification after the presentation.

Practice Active Listening Skills in Conversation

Most people have had the experience of being in a one-way conversation in which one person does all the talking and the others just listen. In fact, this is not a conversation, which is by definition an exchange of information and ideas. In a true conversation, everyone has a chance to be heard. Do not monopolize conversation. Give the other person or persons an opportunity to talk. Pay attention when others are speaking and show your interest in what is being said by making eye contact and asking questions. Avoid interrupting since this shows your disinterest and also suggests that what you have to say is more important.

Case Study

Part 1

You work for the local chamber of commerce and are responsible for assisting the office manager, Teresa Alexander. Ms. Alexander would like to maintain consistency in articles submitted for publication in the monthly chamber newsletter. She wants you to explore various decorative and plain fonts. She would like you to choose two handwriting fonts, two decorative fonts, and two plain fonts and then prepare a document containing an example of each font. Save the document and name it **2-Fonts**. Print and then close the document.

Part 2

Ms. Alexander has asked you to write a short article for the upcoming chamber newsletter. In the article, you are to describe an upcoming event at your school, a local college or university, or your community. Effectively use at least two of the fonts you wrote about in the document you prepared for Case Study Part 1. Save the document and name it **2-Article**. Print and then close the document.

Part 3

Ms. Alexander will be posting the newsletter to the chamber's website and would like you to determine how to save a Word document as a web page. Display the Save As dialog box and then determine how to save a document as a filtered web page using the *Save as type* option. Create a Word document describing the steps for saving a document as a filtered web page. Save the document and name it **2-WebPage**. Print and then close the document. Open **2-Article.docx**, the document you created in Case Study Part 2 and then save the document as a filtered web page.

CHAPTER 3

Customizing Paragraphs

Study Tools

Study tools include a presentation and a list of chapter Quick Steps and Hint margin notes. Use these resources to help you further develop and review skills learned in this chapter.

Concepts Check

Check your understanding by identifying application tools used in this chapter. If you are a SNAP user, launch the Concepts Check from your Assignments page..

Recheck

Check your understanding by taking this quiz. If you are a SNAP user, launch the Recheck from your Assignments page.

Skills Exercise

Additional activities are available to SNAP users. If you are a SNAP user, access these activities from your Assignments page.

Skills Assessment

Assessment 1

Data Files

Apply Paragraph Formatting to a Computer Ethics Document

1. Open **CompEthics.docx** and then save it with the name **3-CompEthics**.
2. Move the insertion point to the end of the document and then type the text shown in Figure WB-3.1. Apply bulleted formatting, as shown in the figure.
3. Select the paragraphs in the *Computer Ethics* section and then apply numbered formatting.
4. Select the paragraphs in the *Technology Timeline* section and then apply bulleted formatting.
5. Insert the following paragraph between paragraphs 2 and 3 in the *Computer Ethics* section: Find sources relating to the latest federal and/or state legislation on privacy protection.
6. Apply the Heading 1 style to the three headings in the document.
7. Apply the Shaded style set.
8. Apply the Slice theme.
9. Apply Light Turquoise, Background 2, Lighter 80% paragraph shading (third column, second row) to the numbered paragraphs in the *Computer Ethics* section and the bulleted paragraphs in the *Technology Timeline* and *ACLU Fair Electronic Monitoring Policy* sections.
10. Save, print, and then close **3-CompEthics.docx**.

Figure WB-3.1 Assessment 1

ACLU Fair Electronic Monitoring Policy

- Notice to employees of the company's electronic monitoring practices
- Use of a signal to let an employee know he or she is being monitored
- Employee access to all personal data collected through monitoring
- No monitoring of areas designed for the health or comfort of employees
- The right to dispute and delete inaccurate data
- A ban on the collection of data unrelated to work performance
- Restrictions on the disclosure of personal data to others without the employee's consent

Assessment 2

Data Files

Type Tabbed Text and Apply Formatting to a Computer Software Document

1. Open **ProdSoftware.docx** and then save it with the name **3-ProdSoftware**.
2. Move the insertion point to the end of the document and then set left tabs at the 0.75-inch, 2.75-inch, and 4.5-inch marks on the horizontal ruler. Type the text in Figure WB-3.2 and type the tabbed text at the tabs you set. Use the New Line command after typing each line of text in columns (except the last line).
3. Apply the Heading 1 style to the three headings in the document (*Productivity Software*, *Personal-Use Software*, and *Software Training Schedule*).
4. Apply the Retrospect theme.
5. Select the productivity software categories in the *Productivity Software* section (from *Word processing* through *Computer-aided design*) and then sort the text alphabetically.
6. With the text still selected, apply bulleted formatting.
7. Select the personal-use software categories in the *Personal-Use Software* section (from *Personal finance software* through *Games and entertainment software*) and then sort the text alphabetically.
8. With the text still selected, apply bulleted formatting.
9. Apply to the heading *Productivity Software* a single-line top border and Olive Green, Text 2, Lighter 80% paragraph shading (fourth column, second row).
10. Apply the same single-line top border and olive green shading to the other two headings (*Personal-Use Software* and *Software Training Schedule*).

Figure WB-3.2 Assessment 2

Games and entertainment software: Designed to provide fun as well as challenges to users; includes interactive games, videos, and music.

Software Training Schedule

Word	April 18	8:30 to 11:30 a.m.
PowerPoint	April 26	1:00 to 3:30 p.m.
Excel	May 8	8:30 to 11:30 a.m.
Access	May 10	1:00 to 3:30 p.m.

11. With the insertion point positioned on the first line of tabbed text, move the tab symbols on the horizontal ruler as follows:
    a. Move the tab at the 0.75-inch mark to the 1-inch mark.
    b. Move the tab at the 4.5-inch mark to the 4-inch mark.
12. Save, print, and then close **3-ProdSoftware.docx**.

Assessment 3 Type and Format a Table of Contents Document

1. At a new blank document, type the document shown in Figure WB-3.3 with the following specifications:
    a. Change the font to 11-point Cambria.
    b. Bold and center the title as shown.
    c. Before typing the text in columns, display the Tabs dialog box. Set two left tabs at the 1-inch mark and the 1.5-inch mark and a right tab with period leaders at the 5.5-inch mark.
    d. When typing the text, press the Enter key to end each line of text.
2. Save the document and name it **3-TofC**.
3. Print **3-TofC.docx**.
4. Select the text in columns and then move the tab symbols on the horizontal ruler as follows. (Because you pressed the Enter key instead of Shift + Enter at the end of each line of text, you need to select all the text in the columns before moving the tabs.)
    a. Delete the left tab symbol at the 1.5-inch mark.
    b. Set a new left tab at the 0.5-inch mark.
    c. Move the right tab at the 5.5-inch mark to the 6-inch mark.
5. Insert single-line borders above and below the title *TABLE OF CONTENTS*.
6. Apply Orange, Accent 2, Lighter 80% paragraph shading to the title *TABLE OF CONTENTS*.
7. Save, print, and then close **3-TofC.docx**.

Figure WB-3.3 Assessment 3

TABLE OF CONTENTS

Operating System..2
    User Interface..3
    Configuring Hardware..5
    Controlling Input and Output..7
Software..10
    Productivity Software..12
    Contact Management Software..15
    Entertainment Software..18
    Mobile Applications..20
Review and Assessment..21
Projects..22

Assessment 4

Data Files

Format a Building Construction Agreement Document

1. Open **ConstructAgrmnt.docx** and then save it with the name **3-ConstructAgrmnt**.
2. Select and then delete the paragraph (including the blank line below the paragraph) that begins *Supervision of Work.*
3. Select and then delete the paragraph (including the blank line below the paragraph) that begins *Builder's Right to Terminate the Contract.*
4. Move the paragraph (including the blank line below the paragraph) that begins *Financing Arrangements* above the paragraph that begins *Start of Construction.*
5. Open **AgrmntItems.docx**.
6. Display the Clipboard task pane and then clear all the contents, if necessary.
7. Select and then copy the first paragraph.
8. Select and then copy the second paragraph.
9. Select and then copy the third paragraph.
10. Close **AgrmntItems.docx**.
11. With **3-ConstructAgrmnt.docx** open, display of the Clipboard task pane, paste the *Supervision* paragraph *above* the *Changes and Alterations* paragraph, and then merge the formatting. (Make sure you position the insertion point *above* the paragraph before you paste the text.)
12. Paste the *Pay Review* paragraph *above* the *Possession of Residence* paragraph and then merge the formatting.
13. Clear all items from the Clipboard and then close the Clipboard task pane.
14. Check the spacing between paragraphs. Insert or delete blank lines to maintain consistent spacing.
15. Save, print, and then close **3-ConstructAgrmnt.docx**.

Assessment 5

Data Files

Hyphenate Words in a Report

1. In some Word documents, especially documents with left and right margins wider than 1 inch, the right margin may appear quite ragged. If the paragraph alignment is changed to justified alignment, the right margin will appear even, but there will be extra space added between words throughout the line. In these situations, hyphenating long words that fall at the ends of text lines provides the document with a more balanced look. Click the Layout tab and then explore the options available in the Hyphenation button drop-down list. Figure out how to automatically hyphenate words in a document and how to limit the number of consecutive hyphens using an option at the Hyphenation dialog box.
2. Open **InterfaceApps.docx** and then save it with the name **3-InterfaceApps**.
3. Automatically hyphenate words in the document, limiting the number of consecutive hyphens to two. ***Hint: Display the Hyphenation dialog box by clicking the Hyphenation button in the Page Setup group on the Layout tab and then clicking*** **Hyphenation Options.**
4. Save, print, and then close **3-InterfaceApps.docx**.

Visual Benchmark

Create a Resume

1. At a blank document, click the *No Spacing* style and then type the resume document shown in Figure WB-3.4. Apply character and paragraph formatting as shown in the figure. Insert 6 points of spacing after the headings *PROFESSIONAL EXPERIENCE, EDUCATION, TECHNOLOGY SKILLS,* and *REFERENCES*. Change the font size of the name *DEVON CHAMBERS* to 16 points.
2. Save the document with the name **3-Resume**.
3. Print and then close the document.

Case Study

Part 1

Data Files

You are the assistant to Gina Coletti, manager of La Dolce Vita, an Italian restaurant. She has been working on updating and formatting the lunch menu. She has asked you to complete the menu by opening **Menu.docx**, determining how the appetizer section is formatted, and then applying the same formatting to the sections *Soups and Salads*; *Sandwiches, Calzones and Burgers*; and *Individual Pizzas*. Save the document with the name **3-Menu**. Print and then close the document.

Part 2

Ms. Coletti has reviewed the completed menu and is pleased with it, but she wants to add a border around the entire page to increase visual interest. Open **3-Menu.docx** and then save it with the name **3-MenuPgBorder**. Display the Borders and Shading dialog box with the Page Border tab selected and then experiment with the options available. Apply an appropriate page border to the menu. (Consider applying an art image border.) Save, print, and then close **3-MenuPgBorder.docx**.

Part 3

Data Files

Each week, the restaurant offers daily specials. Ms. Coletti has asked you to open and format the text in **MenuSpecials.docx**. She has asked you to format the specials menu in a similar manner as the main menu but to change some elements so it is unique from the main menu. Apply the same page border to the specials menu document that you applied to the main menu document. Save the document with the name **3-MenuSpecials**. Print and then close the document.

Part 4

You have been asked by the head chef to research a new recipe for an Italian dish. Using the Internet, find a recipe that interests you and then prepare a Word document containing the recipe and ingredients. Bullet the items in the list of ingredients and number the steps in the recipe preparation. Save the document with the name **3-Recipe**. Print and then close the document.

Figure WB-3.4 Visual Benchmark

DEVON CHAMBERS

344 North Anderson Road * Oklahoma City, OK 73177 * (404) 555-3228

PROFILE

Business manager with successful track record at entrepreneurial start-up and strong project management skills. Keen ability to motivate and supervise employees, a strong hands-on experience with customer service, marketing, and operations. Highly organized and motivated professional looking to leverage strengths in leadership and organizational skills in a project coordinator role.

PROFESSIONAL EXPERIENCE

Midwest Deli, Oklahoma City, OK .... 07/16 to present
Assistant Manager

- Coordinated the opening of a new business, which included budgeting start-up costs, establishing relationships with vendors, ordering supplies, purchasing and installing equipment, and marketing the business to the community
- Manage business personnel, which includes recruitment, interviewing, hiring, training, motivating staff, and resolving conflicts
- Manage daily business operations through customer satisfaction, quality control, employee scheduling, process improvement, and product inventory maintenance

Marin Associates, Shawnee, OK ....06/14 to 06/16
Projects Coordinator

- Developed and maintained a secure office network and installed and repaired computers
- Provided support for hardware and software issues
- Directed agency projects such as equipment purchases, office reorganization, and building maintenance and repair

Moore Insurance Agency, Shawnee, OK ....04/12 to 05/14
Administrative Assistant

- Prepared documents and forms for staff and clients
- Organized and maintained paper and electronic files and scheduled meetings and appointments
- Disseminated information using the telephone, mail services, websites, and email

EDUCATION

Associate of Arts, Business 2016
Oklahoma City Community College

TECHNOLOGY SKILLS

- Proficient in Microsoft Word, Excel, and PowerPoint
- Knowledgeable in current and previous versions of the Windows operating system
- Experience with networking, firewalls, and security systems

REFERENCES

Professional and personal references available upon request.

CHAPTER 4

Formatting Pages

Study Tools

Study tools include a presentation and a list of chapter Quick Steps and Hint margin notes. Use these resources to help you further develop and review skills learned in this chapter.

Concepts Check

Check your understanding by identifying application tools used in this chapter. If you are a SNAP user, launch the Concepts Check from your Assignments page..

Recheck

Check your understanding by taking this quiz. If you are a SNAP user, launch the Recheck from your Assignments page.

Skills Exercise

Additional activities are available to SNAP users. If you are a SNAP user, access these activities from your Assignments page.

Skills Assessment

Assessment 1

Data Files

Format a Cover Letter Document and Create a Cover Page

1. Open **CoverLetter.docx** and then save it with the name **4-CoverLetter**.
2. Change the left and right margins to 1.25 inches.
3. Move the insertion point to the beginning of the heading *Writing Cover Letters to People You Know* and then insert a blank page.
4. Insert a page break at the beginning of the heading *Writing Cover Letters to People You Don't Know*.
5. Move the insertion point to the beginning of the document and then insert the Filigree cover page.
6. Insert the following text in the specified fields:
   a. Type job search strategies in the *[DOCUMENT TITLE]* placeholder.
   b. Type Writing a Cover Letter in the *[Document subtitle]* placeholder.
   c. Type february 2, 2018 in the *[DATE]* placeholder.
   d. Type career finders in the *[COMPANY NAME]* placeholder.
   e. Delete the *[Company address]* placeholder.
7. Move the insertion point to anywhere in the title *WRITING A COVER LETTER* and then insert the Brackets 1 page numbering at the bottom of the page. (The page numbering will not appear on the cover page.)
8. Make the document active, turn on the display of nonprinting characters, move the insertion point to the blank line above the page break below the first paragraph of text in the document, and then press the Delete key six times. (This deletes the page break on the first page and the page break creating a blank page 2, as well as extra hard returns.) Turn off the display of nonprinting characters.
9. Save, print, and then close **4-CoverLetter.docx**.

Assessment 2

Data Files

Format an Intellectual Property Report and Insert Headers and Footers

1. Open **PropProtect.docx** and then save it with the name **4-PropProtect**.
2. Insert a page break at the beginning of the title *REFERENCES* (on the second page).
3. Change the top margin to 1.5 inches.
4. Change the page layout to landscape orientation.
5. Move the insertion point to the beginning of the document and then insert the Retrospect footer. Select the name at the left side of the footer and then type your first and last names.
6. Save the document and then print only page 1.
7. Change the page layout back to portrait orientation.
8. Apply the Moderate page margins.
9. Remove the footer.
10. Insert the Ion (Dark) header.
11. Insert the Ion (Dark) footer. Type property protection issues as the title and make sure your first and last names display at the right side of the footer.
12. Select the footer text (document name and your name), apply bold formatting, and then change the font size to 8 points.
13. Insert the DRAFT 1 watermark in the document.
14. Apply the Green, Accent 6, Lighter 80% page background color (last column, second row).
15. Save and then print **4-PropProtect.docx**.
16. With the document still open, change the paper size to Legal (8.5 inches by 14 inches).
17. Save the document with Save As and name it **4-PropProtect-Legal**.
18. Check with your instructor to determine if you can print legal-sized documents. If so, print page 1 of the document.
19. Save and then close **4-PropProtect-Legal.docx**.

Assessment 3

Data Files

Format a Real Estate Agreement

1. Open **REAgrmnt.docx** and then save it with the name **4-REAgrmnt**.
2. Find all occurrences of *BUYER* (matching the case) and replace them with *James Berman*.
3. Find all occurrences of *SELLER* (matching the case) and replace them with *Mona Trammell*.
4. Find all word forms of the word *buy* and replace them with *purchase*.
5. Search for all occurrences of 14-point Tahoma bold formatting in the standard dark red color and replace them with 12-point Constantia bold formatting in Black, Text 1.
6. Insert Plain Number 2 page numbering at the bottom center of the page.
7. Insert a page border with the following specifications:
   - Choose the first double-line border in the *Style* list box.
   - Change the color of the page border to the standard dark red color.
   - Change the width of the page border to 1 1/2 points.
8. Display the Border and Shading Options dialog box and then change the top, left, bottom, and right measurements to 30 points. ***Hint: Display the Border and Shading Options dialog box by clicking the Options button at the Borders and Shading dialog box with the Page Border tab selected.***
9. Save, print, and then close **4-REAgrmnt.docx**.

Visual Benchmark

Data Files

Format a Resume Styles Report

1. Open **Resumes.docx** and then save it with the name **4-Resumes**.
2. Format the document so it appears as shown in Figure WB-4.1 with the following specifications:
   a. Change the top margin to 1.5 inches.
   b. Change the line spacing for the entire document to 1.5 lines.
   c. Apply the Heading 1 style to the title and the Heading 2 style to the headings.
   d. Apply the Lines (Simple) style set.
   e. Apply the Savon theme.
   f. Apply the Blue Green theme colors.
   g. Change the paragraph spacing after the title to 9 points. Apply 6 points of paragraph spacing after the three headings.
   h. Insert the Austin cover page. Insert text in the placeholders and delete the placeholder as shown in the figure. (If a name displays in the author placeholder, delete it and then type your first and last names.)
   i. Insert the Ion (Dark) header and the Ion (Dark) footer.
3. Save, print, and then close **4-Resumes.**

Figure WB-4.1 Visual Benchmark

Figure WB-4.1 Visual Benchmark

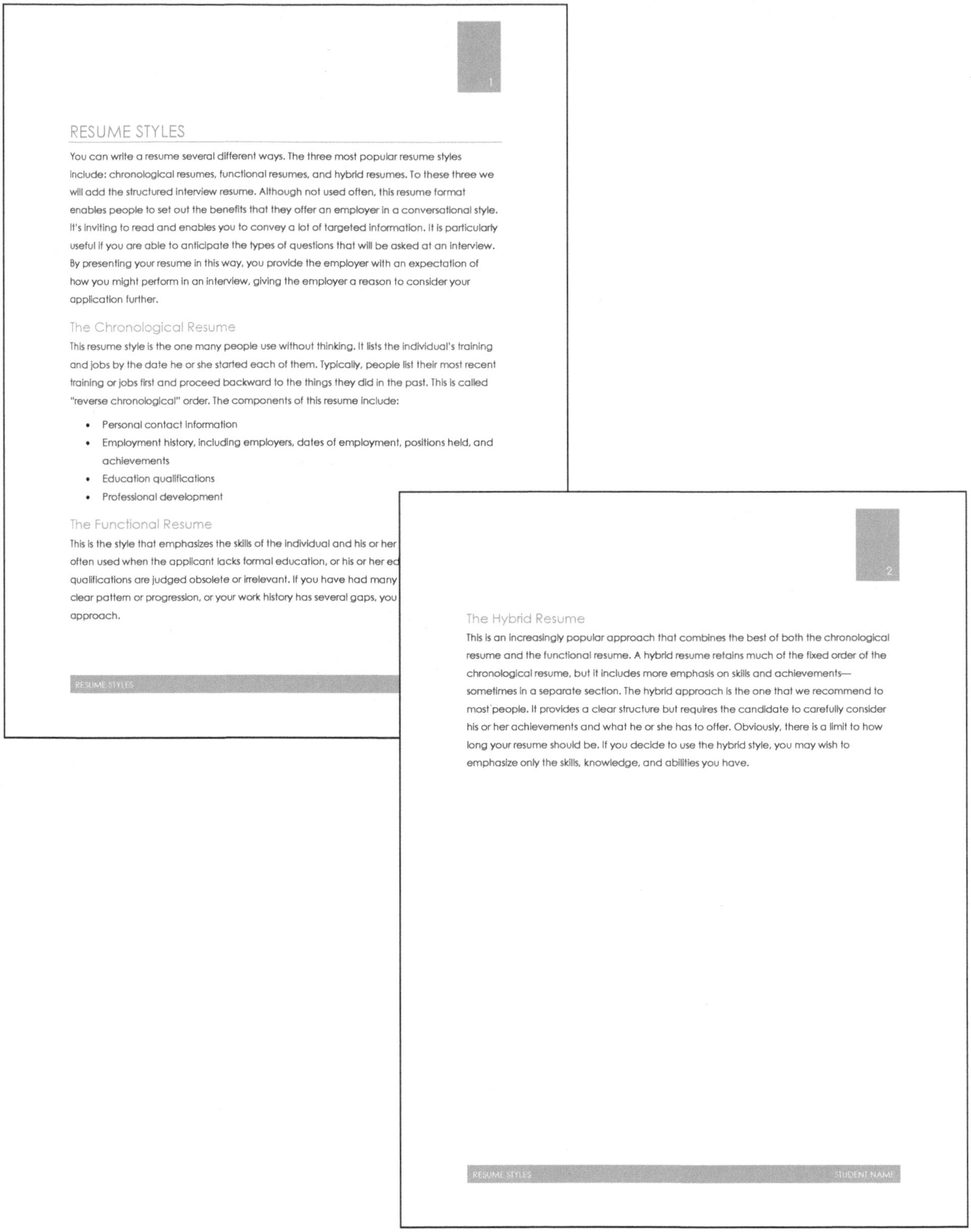

1

RESUME STYLES

You can write a resume several different ways. The three most popular resume styles include: chronological resumes, functional resumes, and hybrid resumes. To these three we will add the structured interview resume. Although not used often, this resume format enables people to set out the benefits that they offer an employer in a conversational style. It's inviting to read and enables you to convey a lot of targeted information. It is particularly useful if you are able to anticipate the types of questions that will be asked at an interview. By presenting your resume in this way, you provide the employer with an expectation of how you might perform in an interview, giving the employer a reason to consider your application further.

The Chronological Resume

This resume style is the one many people use without thinking. It lists the individual's training and jobs by the date he or she started each of them. Typically, people list their most recent training or jobs first and proceed backward to the things they did in the past. This is called "reverse chronological" order. The components of this resume include:

- Personal contact information
- Employment history, including employers, dates of employment, positions held, and achievements
- Education qualifications
- Professional development

The Functional Resume

This is the style that emphasizes the skills of the individual and his or her often used when the applicant lacks formal education, or his or her ed qualifications are judged obsolete or irrelevant. If you have had many clear pattern or progression, or your work history has several gaps, you approach.

RESUME STYLES

2

The Hybrid Resume

This is an increasingly popular approach that combines the best of both the chronological resume and the functional resume. A hybrid resume retains much of the fixed order of the chronological resume, but it includes more emphasis on skills and achievements—sometimes in a separate section. The hybrid approach is the one that we recommend to most people. It provides a clear structure but requires the candidate to carefully consider his or her achievements and what he or she has to offer. Obviously, there is a limit to how long your resume should be. If you decide to use the hybrid style, you may wish to emphasize only the skills, knowledge, and abilities you have.

RESUME STYLES STUDENT NAME

Case Study

Part 1

Data Files

You work for Citizens for Consumer Safety, a nonprofit organization that provides information on household safety. Your supervisor, Melinda Johansson, has asked you to create an attractive document on smoke detectors. She will use the document as an informational handout during a presentation on smoke detectors. Open **SmokeDetectors.docx** and then save it with the name **4-SmokeDetectors-1**. Apply a style set, apply appropriate styles to the title and headings, and then apply a theme. Ms. Johansson has asked you to change the page layout to landscape orientation and to change the left and right margins to 1.5 inches. She wants to allow extra space at the left and right margins so audience members can write notes in these areas. Use the Help feature or experiment with the options in the Header & Footer Tools Design tab and figure out how to number pages on every page but the first page. Insert page numbering in the document that prints at the top right side of every page except the first page. Save, print, and then close **4-SmokeDetectors-1.docx**.

Part 2

Data Files

After reviewing the formatted document on smoke detectors, Ms. Johansson has decided that she would like it to print in the default orientation (portrait) and that she would like to see different theme and style choices. She has also decided that the term *smoke alarm* should be replaced with *smoke detector*. She has asked you to open and then make changes to the original document. Open **SmokeDetectors.docx** and then save it with the name **4-SmokeDetectors-2**. Apply styles to the title and headings and apply a theme to the document (other than the one you chose for Part 1). Search for all occurrences of *Smoke Alarm* and replace them with *Smoke Detector* matching the case. Search for all occurrences of *smoke alarm* and replace them with *smoke detector* without matching the case. Insert a cover page of your choosing and then insert the appropriate information in the page. Use the current date and your name as the author and delete all unused placeholders. Use the Help feature or experiment with the options in the Header & Footer Tools Design tab and figure out how to insert odd-page and even-page footers in a document. Insert an odd-page footer that prints the page number at the right margin and insert an even-page footer that prints the page number at the left margin. You do not want the footer to print on the cover page, so make sure you position the insertion point below the cover page before inserting the footers. Save, print, and then close **4-SmokeDetectors-2.docx**.

Part 3

Ms. Johansson has asked you to prepare a document on infant car seats and car seat safety. She wants this informational car seat safety document to be available for distribution at a local community center. Use the Internet to find websites that provide information on child and infant car seats and car seat safety. Using the information you find, write a report that covers at least the following topics:

- Description of types of car seats (such as rear-facing, convertible, forward-facing, built-in, and booster)
- Safety rules and guidelines
- Installation information
- Specific child and infant seat models
- Sites on the Internet that sell car seats
- Price ranges
- Internet sites that provide safety information

Format the report using styles and a theme and include a cover page and headers and/or footers. Save the completed document and name it **4-CarSeats**. Print and then close the document.

Unit 1 Performance Assessment

Data Files

Before beginning unit work, copy the WL1U1 folder to your storage medium and then make WL1U1 the active folder.

Assessing Proficiency

In this unit, you have learned to create, edit, save, and print Word documents. You have also learned to format characters, paragraphs, and pages.

Assessment 1

Data Files

Format a Document on Website Design

1. Open **Website.docx** and then save it with the name **U1-Website**.
2. Complete a spelling and grammar check.
3. Select the text from the paragraph that begins *Make your home page work for you.* through the end of the document and then apply bulleted formatting.
4. Select and then apply bold formatting to the first sentence of each bulleted paragraph.
5. Apply a single-line bottom border to the document title and apply Gold, Accent 4, Lighter 80% paragraph shading to the title.
6. Save and then print **U1-Website.docx**.
7. Change the top, left, and right margins to 1.5 inches.
8. Select the bulleted paragraphs, change the paragraph alignment to justified, and then apply numbered formatting.
9. Select the entire document and then change the font to 12-point Cambria.
10. Insert the text shown in Figure WB-U1.1 after paragraph number 2. (The number *3.* should be inserted preceding the text you type.)
11. Save, print, and then close **U1-Website.docx**.

Figure WB-U1.1 Assessment 1

Avoid a cluttered look. In design, less is more. Strive for a clean look to your pages, using ample margins and white space.

Assessment 2 — Format an Accumulated Returns Document

Data Files

1. Open **ReturnChart.docx** and then save it with the name **U1-ReturnChart**.
2. Select the entire document and then make the following changes:
   a. Apply the No Spacing style.
   b. Change the line spacing to 1.5 lines.
   c. Change the font to 12-point Cambria.
   d. Apply 6 points of spacing after paragraphs.
3. Select the title *TOTAL RETURN CHARTS*, change the font to 14-point Corbel bold, change the alignment to centered, and apply Blue-Gray, Text 2, Lighter 80% paragraph shading (fourth column, second row in the *Theme Colors* section).
4. Bold the following text that appears at the beginnings of the second through the fifth paragraphs:

   Average annual total return:
   Annual total return:
   Accumulation units:
   Accumulative rates:
5. Select the paragraphs of text in the body of the document (all paragraphs except the title) and then change the paragraph alignment to justified.
6. Select the paragraphs that begin with the bolded words, sort the paragraphs in ascending order, and then indent the text 0.5 inch from the left margin.
7. Insert a watermark that prints *DRAFT* diagonally across the page.
8. Save, print, and then close **U1-ReturnChart.docx**.

Assessment 3 — Format a Computer Ethics Report

Data Files

1. Open **FutureEthics.docx** and then save it with the name **U1-FutureEthics**.
2. Apply the Heading 1 style to the titles *FUTURE OF COMPUTER ETHICS* and *REFERENCES*.
3. Apply the Heading 2 style to the headings in the document.
4. Apply the Shaded style set.
5. Apply the Open paragraph spacing.
6. Apply the Parallax theme and then change the theme fonts to Garamond.
7. Center the two titles (*FUTURE OF COMPUTER ETHICS* and *REFERENCES*).
8. Add 6 points of paragraph spacing after each title and heading with the Heading 1 or Heading 2 style applied.
9. Hang-indent the paragraphs of text below the title *REFERENCES*.
10. Insert page numbering that prints at the bottom center of each page.
11. Save, print, and then close **U1-FutureEthics.docx**.

Assessment 4 — Set Tabs and Type Income by Division Text in Columns

1. At a new blank document, type the text shown in Figure WB-U1.2 with the following specifications:
   a. Apply bold formatting to and center the title as shown.
   b. You determine the tab settings for the text in columns.
   c. Select the entire document and then change the font to 12-point Arial.
2. Save the document with the name **U1-Income**.
3. Print and then close **U1-Income.docx**.

Figure WB-U1.2 Assessment 4

INCOME BY DIVISION

	2016	**2017**	**2018**
Public Relations	$14,375	$16,340	$16,200
Database Services	9,205	15,055	13,725
Graphic Design	18,400	21,790	19,600
Technical Support	5,780	7,325	9,600

Assessment 5

Set Tabs and Type Table of Contents Text

1. At a blank document, type the text shown in Figure WB-U1.3 with the following specifications:
   a. Apply bold formatting to and center the title as shown.
   b. You determine the tab settings for the text in columns.
   c. Select the entire document, change the font to 12-point Cambria, and then change the line spacing to 1.5 lines.
2. Save the document with the name **U1-TofC**.
3. Print and then close **U1-TofC.docx**.

Figure WB-U1.3 Assessment 5

TABLE OF CONTENTS

Online Shopping. 2

Online Services. 4

Peer-to-Peer Online Transactions. 5

Transaction Payment Methods. 8

Transaction Security and Encryption 11

Establishing a Website. 14

Assessment 6

Data Files

Format a Union Agreement Contract

1. Open **LaborContract.docx** and then save it with the name **U1-LaborContract**.
2. Find all occurrences of *REINBERG MANUFACTURING* and replace them with *MILLWOOD ENTERPRISES*.
3. Find all occurrences of *RM* and replace them with *ME*.
4. Find all occurrences of *LABOR WORKERS' UNION* and replace them with *SERVICE EMPLOYEES' UNION*.
5. Find all occurrences of *LWU* and replace them with *SEU*.
6. Select the entire document and then change the font to 12-point Cambria and the line spacing to double spacing.
7. Select the numbered paragraphs in the section *Transfers and Moving Expenses* and change them to bulleted paragraphs.

8. Select the numbered paragraphs in the section *Sick Leave* and change them to bulleted paragraphs.
9. Change to landscape orientation and change the top margin to 1.5 inches.
10. Save and then print **U1-LaborContract.docx**.
11. Change to portrait orientation and the left margin (previously the top margin) back to 1 inch.
12. Insert the Whisp cover page and then insert the current date in the date placeholder, the title *Union Agreement* as the document title, and *Millwood Enterprises* as the document subtitle. Select the author placeholder (or the name) at the bottom of the cover page and then type your first and last names. Delete the company name placeholder.
13. Move the insertion point to the page after the cover page, insert the Ion (Dark) footer, and then make sure *UNION AGREEMENT* displays in the title placeholder and your name displays in the author placeholder. If not, type UNION AGREEMENT in the title placeholder and your first and last names in the author placeholder.
14. Save, print, and then close **U1-LaborContract.docx**.

Assessment 7 Copy and Paste Text in a Health Plan Document

Data Files

1. Open **KeyLifePlan.docx** and then save it with the name **U1-KeyLifePlan**.
2. Open **PlanOptions.docx** and then display the Clipboard task pane. Make sure the Clipboard is empty.
3. Select the heading *Plan Highlights* and the six paragraphs of text below it and then copy the selected text to the Clipboard.
4. Select the heading *Plan Options* and the two paragraphs of text below it (the second paragraph flows onto the next page) and then copy the selected text to the Clipboard.
5. Select the heading *Quality Assessment* and the six paragraphs of text below it and then copy the selected text to the Clipboard.
6. Close **PlanOptions.docx**.
7. With **U1-KeyLifePlan.docx** open, display the Clipboard task pane.
8. Move the insertion point to the beginning of the heading *Provider Network*, paste the *Plan Options* item from the Clipboard, and merge the formatting.
9. With the insertion point positioned at the beginning of the heading *Provider Network*, paste *Plan Highlights* from the Clipboard and merge the formatting.
10. Move the insertion point to the beginning of the heading *Plan Options*, paste the *Quality Assessment* item from the Clipboard, and merge the formatting.
11. Clear the Clipboard and then close it.
12. Apply the Heading 1 style to the title *KEY LIFE HEALTH PLAN*.
13. Apply the Heading 2 style to the four headings in the document.
14. Change the top margin to 1.5 inches.
15. Apply the Lines (Simple) style set.
16. Apply the Compact paragraph spacing.
17. Apply the Red Orange theme colors.
18. Insert a double-line page border in the standard dark red color.
19. Insert the Slice 1 header.
20. Insert the Slice footer and type your first and last names in the author placeholder.
21. Insert a page break at the beginning of the heading *Plan Highlights*.
22. Save, print, and then close **U1-KeyLifePlan.docx**.

Assessment 8

Create and Format a Resume

1. Click the File tab, click the *New* option, and then double-click the *Single spaced (blank)* template. At the blank document, create the resume shown in Figure WB-U1.4. Change the font to Candara and apply the character, paragraph, border, shading, and bulleted formatting as shown in the figure.
2. Save the completed document with the name **U1-Resume**.
3. Print and then close **U1-Resume.docx**.

Figure WB-U1.4 Assessment 8

KIERNAN O'MALLEY

1533 Baylor Street East, Auburn, WA 98020 (253) 555-3912

NETWORK ADMINISTRATION PROFESSIONAL
Pursuing **CCNA Cloud certification** and **Network+** credentials
Proficient in Microsoft Office applications in Windows environment

EDUCATION

Information Systems (IS), Western Washington University, Bellingham, WA...................... 2015
Medical Specialist, Seattle University, Seattle, WA ....2013 to 2015
Medical Terminology, Green River Community College, Auburn, WA................................. 2012

APPLIED RESEARCH PROJECTS

Completed **Applied Research Projects (ARPs),** in conjunction with IS degree requirements, covering all aspects of design and management of organizational technical resources, as follows:

- **Organizational Culture and Leadership** (2018): Evaluated the organizational culture of Bellevue Surgery Center's endoscopy unit and operating room (OR) in order to ensure that the mission and vision statements were being appropriately applied at the staff level.
- **Human Resources (HR) Management** (2018): Established a comprehensive orientation package for the Bellevue Surgery Center's clinical staff.
- **Strategic Management and Planning** (2017): Conducted internal/external environmental assessments in order to identify an approach for Bellevue Surgery Center to expand its OR facilities.
- **Financial Accounting** (2017): Created a quarterly operating budget for the Bellevue Surgery Center and implemented an expenditure tracking system.
- **Database Management Systems** (2016): Created an inventory-control system that optimizes inventory maintenance in a cost-effective manner.
- **Statistics and Research Analysis** (2016): Generated graphics to illustrate the Valley Hospital's assisted-reproduction success rate.
- **Management Support System** (2015): Identified solutions to resolve inventory-control vulnerabilities at minimal cost for Valley Hospital.

PROFESSIONAL EXPERIENCE

CERTIFIED SURGICAL TECHNOLOGIST

Bellevue Surgery Center, Bellevue, WA...2016 to present
Valley Hospital, Renton, WA .... 2014 to 2016
Kenmore Ambulatory Surgery Center, Kenmore, WA .... 2012 to 2014
South Sound Medical Center, Auburn, WA.. 2011 to 2012

Writing Activities

The following activities give you the opportunity to practice your writing skills along with demonstrating an understanding of some of the important Word features you have mastered in this unit. Use correct grammar, appropriate word choices, and clear sentence construction. Follow the steps in Figure WB-U1.5 to improve your writing skills.

Activity 1

Write Steps on Using KeyTips

Use Word's Help feature to learn about KeyTips. To do this, press the F1 function key to open the Word Help window, type keytips, and then press the Enter key. Click the Keyboard shortcuts for Microsoft Word 2016 for Windows article hyperlink. Scroll down the article and then click the Navigate the ribbon with access keys hyperlink below the heading *In this article*. Read the information about accessing any command with a few keystrokes. (Read only the information in the section *Navigate the ribbon with only the keyboard*.)

At a blank document, write a paragraph summarizing the information you read in the Word Help article. After writing the paragraph, add steps on how to use KeyTips to accomplish the following tasks:

- Turn on bold formatting.
- Display the Font dialog box.
- Print the open document.

Save the completed document with the name **U1-KeyTips**. Print and then close **U1-KeyTips.docx**.

Activity 2

Write Information on Advanced Word Options

Use Word's Help feature and the search text *word options advanced* to learn how to customize display options at the Word Options dialog box with the *Advanced* option selected. After learning about the display options, create a document that describes the steps to change the display of the *Show this number of Recent Documents* option to *10*. Assume that the steps begin at a blank document. Describe the steps to turn on the *Quickly access this number of Recent Documents* option and change the number to *6*. Again, assume that the steps begin at a blank document. Add any additional information such as a title, heading, and/or explanatory text, that helps the reader understand the contents of the document. Save the completed document and name it **U1-DisplayOptions**. Print and then close **U1-DisplayOptions.docx**.

Figure WB-U1.5 The Writing Process

The Writing Process

Plan Gather ideas, select which information to include, and choose the order in which to present the information.

Checkpoints
- What is the purpose?
- What information does the reader need to reach your intended conclusion?

Write Following the information plan and keeping the reader in mind, draft the document using clear, direct sentences that say what you mean.

Checkpoints
- What subpoints support each main thought?
- How can you connect paragraphs so the reader moves smoothly from one idea to the next?

Revise Improve what is written by changing, deleting, rearranging, or adding words, sentences, and paragraphs.

Checkpoints
- Is the meaning clear?
- Do the ideas follow a logical order?
- Have you included any unnecessary information?
- Have you built your sentences around strong nouns and verbs?

Edit Check spelling, sentence construction, word use, punctuation, and capitalization.

Checkpoints
- Can you spot any redundancies or clichés?
- Can you reduce any phrases to an effective word (for example, change *the fact that* to *because*)?
- Have you used commas only where there is a strong reason for doing so?
- Did you proofread the document for errors that your spelling checker cannot identify?

Publish Prepare a final copy that can be reproduced and shared with others.

Checkpoints
- Which design elements, such as bold formatting and different fonts, will help highlight important ideas or sections?
- Will charts or other graphics help clarify meaning?

Internet Research

Research Business Desktop Computer Systems

You hold a part-time job at the local chamber of commerce, where you assist the office manager, Ryan Woods. Mr. Woods will be purchasing new desktop computers for the office staff. He has asked you to research on the Internet and identify at least three PCs that can be purchased directly over the Internet, and he wants you to put your research and recommendations in writing. Mr. Woods is looking for solid, reliable, economical, and powerful desktop computers with good warranties and service plans. He has given you a budget of $800 per unit.

Search the Internet for three desktop PC systems from three different manufacturers. Consider price, specifications (processor speed, amount of RAM, hard drive space, and monitor type and size), performance, warranties, and service plans when choosing the systems. Print your research findings and include them with your report.

Using Word, write a brief report in which you summarize the capabilities and qualities of each of the three computer systems you recommend. Include a final paragraph detailing which system you suggest for purchase and why. If possible, incorporate user opinions and/or reviews about this system to support your decision. Format your report using the concepts and techniques you learned in Unit 1. Save the report with the name **U1-InternetResearch**. Print and then close the file.

Microsoft®

Word Level 1

Unit 2

Enhancing and Customizing Documents

Microsoft® Word

Applying Formatting and Inserting Objects

CHAPTER 5

Study Tools

Study tools include a presentation and a list of chapter Quick Steps and Hint margin notes. Use these resources to help you further develop and review skills learned in this chapter.

Concepts Check

Check your understanding by identifying application tools used in this chapter. If you are a SNAP user, launch the Concepts Check from your Assignments page..

Recheck

Check your understanding by taking this quiz. If you are a SNAP user, launch the Recheck from your Assignments page.

Skills Exercise

Additional activities are available to SNAP users. If you are a SNAP user, access these activities from your Assignments page.

Skills Assessment

Assessment 1

Data Files

Add Visual Appeal to a Report on Intellectual Property

1. Open **ProtectIssues.docx** and then save it with the name **5-ProtectIssues**.
2. Format the text from the first paragraph of text below the title to the end of the document into two columns with 0.4 inch between columns.
3. Move the insertion point to the end of the document and then insert a continuous section break to balance the columns on the second page.
4. Press Ctrl + Home to move the insertion point to the beginning of the document.
5. Insert the image **Hacker.png**. (Do this by clicking the Pictures button on the Insert tab.)
6. Customize the image using these specifications:
   a. Change the height to 1 inch.
   b. Change the color of the image to Blue, Accent color 1 Light (second column, third row in the *Recolor* section).
   c. Correct the contrast to Brightness: 0% (Normal) Contrast: +20% (third column, fourth row in the *Brightness/Contract* section).
   d. Change the position of the image to Position in Middle Left with Square Text Wrapping (first column, second row in the *With Text Wrapping* section).
   e. Using the Rotate Objects button in the Arrange group, flip the image horizontally.
7. Move the insertion point to the beginning of the paragraph immediately below the heading *Intellectual Property Protection* (on the second page). Insert the Austin Quote text box and then make the following customizations:
   a. Type the following text in the text box: "Plagiarism may be punished by law, and in many educational institutions it can result in suspension or even expulsion."

b. Select the text and then change the font size to 11 points.
c. Change the width of the text box to 2.8 inches.
d. Change the position of the text box to Position in Top Center with Square Text Wrapping (second column, first row in the With Text Wrapping section).

8. Press Ctrl + End to move the insertion point to the end of the document. (The insertion point will be positioned below the continuous section break you inserted on the second page to balance the columns of text.)
9. Change the formatting back to one column.
10. Press the Enter key two times and then insert a shape near the insertion point using the Plaque shape (tenth column, second row in the *Basic Shapes* section) and make the following customizations:
    a. Change the shape height to 1.4 inches and the shape width to 3.9 inches.
    b. Use the Align button in the Arrange group to distribute the shape horizontally.
    c. Apply the Subtle Effect - Blue, Accent 1 shape style (second column, fourth row).
    d. Type the text Felicité Compagnie inside the shape. Insert the *é* symbol at the Symbol dialog box with the *(normal text)* font selected.
    e. Insert the current date below *Felicité Compagnie* and insert the current time below the date.
    f. Select the text in the shape, change the font size to 14 points, and apply bold formatting.
11. Manually hyphenate the document. (Do not hyphenate headings and proper names.)
12. Create a drop cap with the first letter of the word *The* that begins the first paragraph of text below the title.
13. Save, print, and then close **5-ProtectIssues.docx**.

Assessment 2 — Create a Sales Meeting Announcement

Data Files

1. At a blank document, press the Enter key two times and then create WordArt with the following specifications:
    a. Apply the Fill - Black, Text 1, Outline - Background 1, Hard Shadow - Background 1 WordArt style (first column, third row) and then type Inlet Corporation in the WordArt text box.
    b. Change the width of the WordArt text box to 6.5 inches.
    c. Use the *Transform* option from the Text Effects button in the WordArt Styles group to apply the Chevron Up text effect (first column, second row in the *Warp* section).
2. Press Ctrl + End and then press the Enter key three times. Change the font to 18-point Candara, apply bold formatting, change to center alignment, and then type the following text, pressing the Enter key after each line of text except the fourth line:

    National Sales Meeting
    Northwest Division
    Ocean View Resort
    August 15 through August 17, 2018

3. Insert the image **Ocean.jpg** and then make the following changes to the image:
    a. Change the width of the image to 6.5 inches.
    b. Apply the Brightness: +40% Contrast: -40% correction (last column, first row in the *Brightness/Contrast* section).
    c. Apply the Compound Frame, Black picture style (fourth column, second row in the pictures styles gallery).

d. Change the position of the image to Position in Top Center with Square Text Wrapping (second column, first row in the *With Text Wrapping* section).
e. Change text wrapping to Behind Text.

4. Save the announcement document and name it **5-SalesMtg**.
5. Print and then close **5-SalesMtg.docx**.

Assessment 3

Data Files

Create an Announcement

1. Open **FirstAidCourse.docx** and then save it with the name **5-FirstAidCourse**.
2. Format the announcement as shown in Figure WB-5.1. Use the Pictures button on the Insert tab to insert the image **FirstAid.png** with the following specifications:
   a. Change the text wrapping to Tight.
   b. Change the image color to Blue, Accent color 5 Light (sixth column, third row in the *Recolor* section).
   c. Correct the brightness and contrast to Brightness: 0% (Normal) Contrast: +40% (third column, bottom row in the *Brightness/Contrast* section).
   d. Size and move the image as shown in the figure.

Figure WB-5.1 Assessment 3

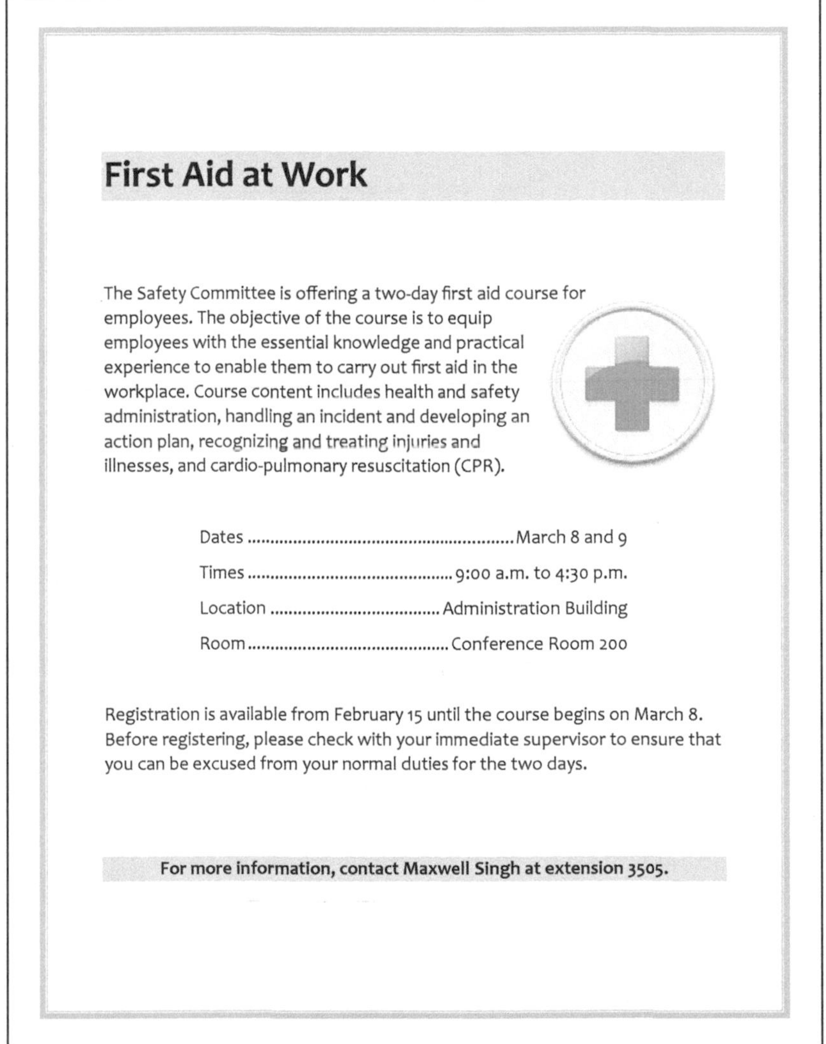

First Aid at Work

The Safety Committee is offering a two-day first aid course for employees. The objective of the course is to equip employees with the essential knowledge and practical experience to enable them to carry out first aid in the workplace. Course content includes health and safety administration, handling an incident and developing an action plan, recognizing and treating injuries and illnesses, and cardio-pulmonary resuscitation (CPR).

Dates .... March 8 and 9
Times .... 9:00 a.m. to 4:30 p.m.
Location .... Administration Building
Room .... Conference Room 200

Registration is available from February 15 until the course begins on March 8. Before registering, please check with your immediate supervisor to ensure that you can be excused from your normal duties for the two days.

For more information, contact Maxwell Singh at extension 3505.

3. Apply paragraph shading, insert the page border, and add period leaders to the tabs, as shown in Figure WB-5.1.
4. Save, print, and then close **5-FirstAidCourse.docx**. (If some of the page border does not print, consider increasing the measurements at the Border and Shading Options dialog box.)

Assessment 4

Data Files

Insert Screenshots in a Memo

1. Open **FirstAidMemo.docx** and then save it with the name **5-FirstAidMemo**.
2. Insert screen clippings so your document appears as shown in Figure WB-5.2. Use the **FirstAidAnnounce.docx** to create the first screen clipping, and use the document **5-FirstAidCourse.docx** you created in Assessment 3 for the second screen clipping. ***Hint: Decrease the display percentage of the document so the entire document is visible on the screen.***
3. Move the insertion point below the screen clipping images and then insert the text as shown in the figure. Insert your initials in place of the *XX*.
4. Save, print, and close **5-FirstAidMemo.docx**.

Figure WB-5.2 Assessment 4

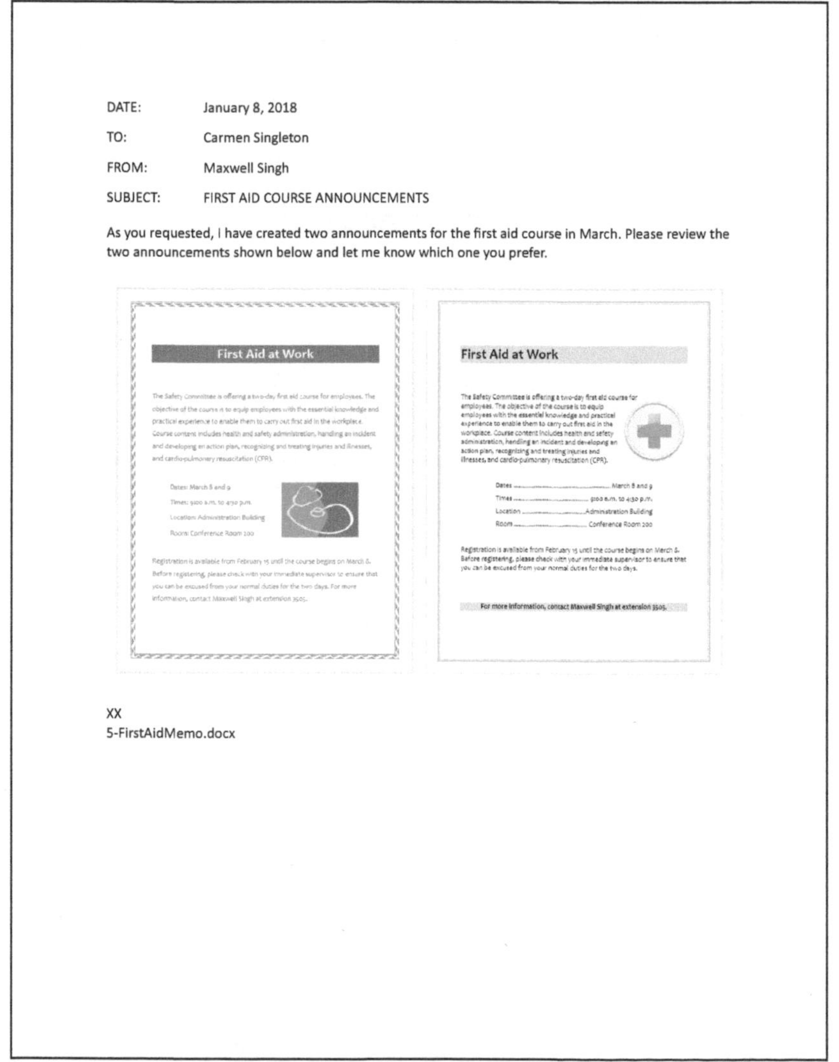

DATE: January 8, 2018

TO: Carmen Singleton

FROM: Maxwell Singh

SUBJECT: FIRST AID COURSE ANNOUNCEMENTS

As you requested, I have created two announcements for the first aid course in March. Please review the two announcements shown below and let me know which one you prefer.

First Aid at Work

First Aid at Work

XX

5-FirstAidMemo.docx

Visual Benchmark

Part 1

Data Files

Create a flyer

1. Create the flyer shown in Figure WB-5.3 with the following specifications:
   - Create the title *Pugs on Parade!* as WordArt using the *Fill - Black, Text 1, Shadow* option. Change the width to 6.5 inches, apply the Can Up transform effect, and change the text fill color to standard dark red.
   - Create the shape containing the text *Admission is free!* using the Explosion 1 shape in the *Stars and Banners* section of the Shapes button drop-down list.
   - Insert the **Pug.jpg** image. (Use the Pictures button on the Insert tab.) Change the text wrapping for the image to Behind Text and size and position the image as shown in the figure.
   - Create the line above the last line of text as a top border. Change the color to standard dark red and the width to 3 points.
   - Make any other changes so your document appears similar to Figure WB-5.3.
2. Save the document and name it **5-PugFlyer**.
3. Print and then close the document.

Figure WB-5.3 Visual Benchmark 1

Part

2

Data Files

Format a Report

1. Open **Resume.docx** and then save it with the name **5-Resume**.
2. Format the report so it appears as shown in Figure WB-5.4 with the following specifications:
   a. Insert the WordArt text *Résumé Writing* with the following specifications:
      - Use the *Fill - Black, Text 1, Outline - Background 1, Hard Shadow - Background 1* option.
      - Type the text Résumé Writing and insert the *é* symbol using the Insert Symbol dialog box.
      - Change the position to Position in Top Center with Square Text Wrapping.
      - Change the width of the WordArt to 5.5 inches.
      - Apply the Can Up transform text effect.

   b. Format the report into two columns beginning with the first paragraph of text below the title and balance the columns on the second page.
   c. Insert the pull quote with the following specifications:
      - Use the Motion Quote text box.
      - Type the text shown in the pull quote in Figure WB-5.4. (Use the Symbol dialog box to insert the two *é* symbols in the word *résumé*.)
      - Select the text and then change the font size to 11 points.
      - Change the width of the text box to 2.3 inches.
      - Position the pull quote as shown in Figure WB-5.4.

   d. Insert the cake image with the following specifications:
      - Insert the **Cake.png** image. (Use the Pictures button on the Insert tab.)
      - Change the image color to Black and White: 50%.
      - Change the width to 0.9 inches.
      - Change the text wrapping to Tight.
      - Position the cake image as shown in Figure WB-5.4.

   e. Insert page numbering at the bottom center of each page with the *Thick Line* option.
3. Save, print, and then close **5-Resume.docx**.

Figure WB-5.4 Visual Benchmark 2

potentially very useful, but do not imagine that is the end of it!

Information about the Job

You should tailor the information in your résumé to the main points in the job advertisement. Get as much information about the job and the company as you can. The main sources of information about a job are normally the following:

- A job advertisement
- A job description
- A friend in the company
- Someone already doing the job or
- The media
- Gossip and rumor

There is no substitute for experience. Talking to someone who does a job similar to the one you wish to apply for in the same company may well provide you with a good picture of what the job is really like. Bear in mind, of course, that this source of information is not always reliable. You may react differently than that person does, and therefore his or her experience with a company may be very different from yours. However, someone with reliable information can provide a golden opportunity. Make sure you do not waste the chance to get some information.

Résumé Writing

To produce the best "fitting" résumé, you need to know about yourself and you need to know about the job you are applying for. Before you do anything else, ask yourself why you are preparing a résumé. The answer to this question is going to vary from one person to the next, and here are our top ten reasons for writing a résumé:

1. You have seen a job that appeals to you advertised in the paper.
2. You want to market yourself to win a contract or a proposal, or be elected to a committee or organization.
3. You have seen a job that appeals to you on an Internet job site.
4. Your friends or family told you of a job opening at a local company.
5. You want to work for the local company and thought that sending a résumé to them might get their attention.
6. You have seen a job advertised internally at work.
7. You are going for a promotion.
8. You are feeling fed up, and writing down all your achievements will cheer you up and might motivate you to look for a better job.
9. You are thinking "Oh, so that's a résumé! I suppose I ought to try to remember what I've been doing with my life."
10. You are about to be downsized and want to update your résumé to be ready for any good opportunities.

"Updating your résumé from time to time is a good idea so you do not forget important details..."

All of these certainly are good reasons to write a résumé, but the résumé serves many different purposes. One way of seeing the different purposes is to ask yourself who is going to read the résumé in each case.

Résumés 1 through 5 will be read by potential employers who probably do not know you. Résumés 6 and 7 are likely to be read by your boss or other people who know you. Résumés 8 through 10 are really for your own benefit and should not be considered as suitable for sending out to employers.

The Right Mix

Think about the list of reasons again. How else can you divide up these reasons? An important difference is that, in some cases, you will have a good idea of what the employer is looking for because you have a job advertisement in front of you and can tailor your résumé accordingly. For others, you have no idea what the reader might want to see. Updating your résumé from time to time is a good idea so you do not forget important details, but remember that the result of such a process will not be a winning résumé. It will be a useful list of tasks and achievements.

Writing a résumé is like baking a cake. You need all the right ingredients: flour, butter, eggs, and so on. It is what you do with the ingredients that makes the difference between a great résumé (or cake) and failure.

Keeping your résumé up-to-date is like keeping a stock of ingredients in the pantry—it's

1

Case Study

Part 1

Data Files

You work for Honoré Financial Services and have been asked by the office manager, Jason Monroe, to prepare an information newsletter. Mr. Monroe has asked you to open the document named **Budget.docx** and then format it into columns. You are to decide the number of columns and any additional enhancements to the columns. Mr. Monroe also wants you to proofread the document and correct any spelling and grammatical errors. Save the completed newsletter, naming it **5-Budget**, and then print it. When Mr. Monroe reviews the newsletter, he decides that it needs additional visual appeal. He wants you to insert visual elements in the newsletter, such as WordArt, an image, a predesigned text box, and/or a drop cap. After adding the element(s), save, print, and then close **5-Budget.docx**.

Part 2

Honoré Financial Services will offer a free workshop titled *Planning for Financial Success*. Mr. Monroe has asked you to prepare an announcement containing information on the workshop. You determine what to include in the announcement, such as the date, time, location, and so forth. Enhance the announcement by inserting an image and by applying formatting such as font, paragraph alignment, and borders. Save the completed document and name it **5-Announce**. Print and then close the document.

Part 3

Honoré Financial Services has adopted a new slogan and Mr. Monroe has asked you to create a shape with the new slogan inside it. Experiment with the shadow and 3-D shape effects available on the Drawing Tools Format tab and then create a shape and enhance it with shadow and/or 3-D effects. Insert the new Honoré Financial Services slogan *Retirement Planning Made Easy* in the shape. Include any additional enhancements to improve the visual appeal of the shape and slogan. Save the completed document and name it **5-Slogan**. Print and then close the document.

Part 4

Mr. Monroe has asked you to prepare a document containing information on teaching children how to budget. Use the Internet to find websites and articles that provide information on this topic. Write a synopsis of the information and include at least four suggestions for teaching children to manage their money. Format the text into newspaper columns. Add additional enhancements to improve the appearance of the document. Save the completed document and name it **5-ChildBudget**. Print and then close the document.

Microsoft® Word

Maintaining Documents and Printing Envelopes and Labels

CHAPTER 6

Study Tools

Study tools include a presentation and a list of chapter Quick Steps and Hint margin notes. Use these resources to help you further develop and review skills learned in this chapter.

Concepts Check

Check your understanding by identifying application tools used in this chapter. If you are a SNAP user, launch the Concepts Check from your Assignments page..

Recheck

Check your understanding by taking this quiz. If you are a SNAP user, launch the Recheck from your Assignments page.

Skills Exercise

Additional activities are available to SNAP users. If you are a SNAP user, access these activities from your Assignments page.

Skills Assessment

Assessment 1

Data Files

Manage Documents

Note: If you downloaded the WL1C6 folder to your storage medium at the beginning of Chapter 6, you have the necessary files to complete the assessments. If you do not have access to the WL1C6 folder, use the ebook Links button to download the WL1C6-WB folder that contains the files needed to complete the assessments. If you are using your OneDrive, please check with your instructor before completing this assessment.

1. Display the Open dialog box with WL1C6 (or WL1C6-WB) on your storage medium the active folder and then create a new folder named *CheckingTools*.
2. Copy (be sure to copy and not cut) both documents that begin with *SpellGrammar* into the CheckingTools folder.
3. With the CheckingTools folder as the active folder, rename **SpellGrammar01.docx** to Technology.
4. Rename **SpellGrammar02.docx** to Software.
5. Capture the Open dialog box as an image file by completing the following steps:
   a. With the Open dialog box displayed, press Alt + Print Screen.
   b. Close the Open dialog box.
   c. If necessary, press Ctrl + N to display a blank document and then click the Paste button.
   d. Print the document.
   e. Close the document without saving it.
6. Display the Open dialog box and make WL1C6 (or WL1C6-WB) on your storage medium the active folder.

7. Delete the CheckingTools folder and all the documents contained within it.
8. Open **StaffMtg.docx**, **Agreement.docx**, and **Robots.docx**.
9. Make **Agreement.docx** the active document.
10. Make **StaffMtg.docx** the active document.
11. Arrange all the windows.
12. Make **Robots.docx** the active document and then minimize it.
13. Minimize the remaining documents.
14. Restore **StaffMtg.docx**.
15. Restore **Agreement.docx**.
16. Restore **Robots.docx**.
17. Maximize and then close **StaffMtg.docx** and then maximize and close **Robots.docx**.
18. Maximize **Agreement.docx** and then save the document with the name **6-Agreement**.
19. Open **AptLease.docx**.
20. View **6-Agreement.docx** and **AptLease.docx** side by side.
21. Scroll through both documents simultaneously and notice the formatting differences between the titles, headings, and fonts in the two documents. Change the font and apply shading to only the title and headings in **6-Agreement.docx** to match the font and shading of the title and headings in **AptLease.docx**.
22. Make **AptLease.docx** active and then close it.
23. Save **6-Agreement.docx**.
24. Move the insertion point to the end of the document and then insert the document named **Terms.docx**.
25. Apply formatting to the inserted text so it matches the formatting of the text in **6-Agreement.docx**.
26. Move the insertion point to the end of the document and then insert the document named **Signature.docx**.
27. Save, print, and then close **6-Agreement.docx**.

Assessment 2 Create an Envelope

1. At a blank document, create an envelope with the text shown in Figure WB-6.1.
2. Save the envelope document and name it **6-EnvMiller**.
3. Print and then close **6-EnvMiller.docx**.

Figure WB-6.1 Assessment 2

DR ROSEANNE HOLT
21330 CEDAR DR
LOGAN UT 84598

GENE MILLER
4559 CORRIN AVE
SMITHFIELD UT 84521

Assessment 3

Create Mailing Labels

1. Create mailing labels with the names and addresses shown in Figure WB-6.2. Use a label option of your choosing. (You may need to check with your instructor before choosing an option.) When entering a street number such as *147TH*, Word will convert the *th* to superscript letters when you press the spacebar after typing *147TH*. To remove the superscript formatting, immediately click the Undo button on the Quick Access Toolbar.
2. Save the document and name it **6-LabelsOhio**.
3. Print and then close **6-LabelsOhio.docx**.
4. At the blank document screen, close the document without saving changes.

Figure WB-6.2 Assessment 3

SUSAN LUTOVSKY 1402 MELLINGER DR FAIRHOPE OH 43209	JIM AND PAT KEIL 413 JACKSON ST AVONDALE OH 43887	IRENE HAGEN 12930 147TH AVE E CANTON OH 43296
VINCE KILEY 14005 288TH ST CANTON OH 43287	LEONARD KRUEGER 13290 N 120TH CANTON OH 43291	HELGA GUNDSTROM PO BOX 3112 AVONDALE OH 43887

Assessment 4

Prepare a Fax

1. Display the New backstage area, search for *fax*, download the Fax (Equity theme) template, and then insert the following information in the specified fields:

To	Frank Gallagher
From	(your first and last names)
Fax	(206) 555-9010
Pages	3
Phone	(206) 555-9005
Date	(insert current date)
Re	Consultation Agreement
CC	Jolene Yin

   Type X in the *For Review* check box.

   Comments Please review the Consultation Agreement and advise me of any legal issues.
2. Save the fax document and name it **6-Fax**.
3. Print and then close the document.

Assessment 5

Data Files

Save a Document as a Web Page

1. Experiment with the *Save as type* option box at the Save As dialog box and figure out how to save a document as a single-file web page.
2. Open **NSS.docx**, display the Save As dialog box, and then change the *Save as type* option to *Single File Web Page (*.mht,*.mhtml)*. Click the Change Title button in the Save As dialog box. At the Enter Text dialog box, type Northland Security Systems in the *Page title* text box and then close the dialog box by clicking the OK button. Click the Save button in the Save As dialog box.

3. Close the **NSS.mht** file.
4. Open your web browser and then open the **NSS.mht** file. (If necessary, check with your instructor to determine the specific steps on opening the web browser and opening the file.)
5. Close your web browser.

Assessment 6

Create Personal Mailing Labels

1. At a blank document, type your name and address and then apply formatting to enhance the appearance of the text. (You determine the font, font size, and font color.)
2. Create labels with your name and address. (You determine the label vendor and product number.)
3. Save the label document and name it **6-PersonalLabels**.
4. Print and then close the document.
5. Close the document containing your name and address without saving the changes.

Assessment 7

Download and Complete a Student Award Certificate

1. Display the New backstage area and then search for and download a student-of-the-month award certificate template. (Type certificate for student of the month in the search text box and then download the Basic certificate for student-of-the-month template. If this template is not available, choose another student of the month award template.)
2. Insert the appropriate information in the award template placeholders, identifying yourself as the recipient of the student-of-the-month award.
3. Save the completed award and name the document **6-Award**.
4. Print and then close the document.

Visual Benchmark

Part 1

Data Files

Create Custom Labels

1. You can create a sheet of labels with the same information in each label by typing the information in the *Address* text box at the Envelopes and Labels dialog box. Or you can type the information, select it, and then create the label. Using this technique, create the sheet of labels shown in Figure WB-6.3 with the following specifications:
   - Open **NSSLabels.docx**.
   - Set the text in 12-point Magneto.
   - Select the entire document and then create the labels using the Avery US Letter label vendor and the 5161 product number.
2. Save the labels document and name it **6-NSSLabels**.
3. Print and then close the document.
4. Close **NSSLabels.docx** without saving it.

Part 2

Create an Invitation

1. At the New backstage area, search for *movie awards party invitation* and then download the template document shown in Figure WB-6.4. (The template does not include the background image of the movie reel.)
2. Apply bold formatting to the text below the heading *Hooray for Hollywood!*.

Figure WB-6.3 Visual Benchmark 1

Northland Security Systems
3200 North 22nd Street
Springfield, IL 62102

Northland Security Systems
3200 North 22nd Street
Springfield, IL 62102

Northland Security Systems
3200 North 22nd Street
Springfield, IL 62102

Northland Security Systems
3200 North 22nd Street
Springfield, IL 62102

Northland Security Systems
3200 North 22nd Street
Springfield, IL 62102

Northland Security Systems
3200 North 22nd Street
Springfield, IL 62102

Northland Security Systems
3200 North 22nd Street
Springfield, IL 62102

Northland Security Systems
3200 North 22nd Street
Springfield, IL 62102

Northland Security Systems
3200 North 22nd Street
Springfield, IL 62102

Northland Security Systems
3200 North 22nd Street
Springfield, IL 62102

Northland Security Systems
3200 North 22nd Street
Springfield, IL 62102

Northland Security Systems
3200 North 22nd Street
Springfield, IL 62102

Northland Security Systems
3200 North 22nd Street
Springfield, IL 62102

Northland Security Systems
3200 North 22nd Street
Springfield, IL 62102

Northland Security Systems
3200 North 22nd Street
Springfield, IL 62102

Northland Security Systems
3200 North 22nd Street
Springfield, IL 62102

Northland Security Systems
3200 North 22nd Street
Springfield, IL 62102

Northland Security Systems
3200 North 22nd Street
Springfield, IL 62102

Northland Security Systems
3200 North 22nd Street
Springfield, IL 62102

Northland Security Systems
3200 North 22nd Street
Springfield, IL 62102

Figure WB-6.4 Visual Benchmark 2

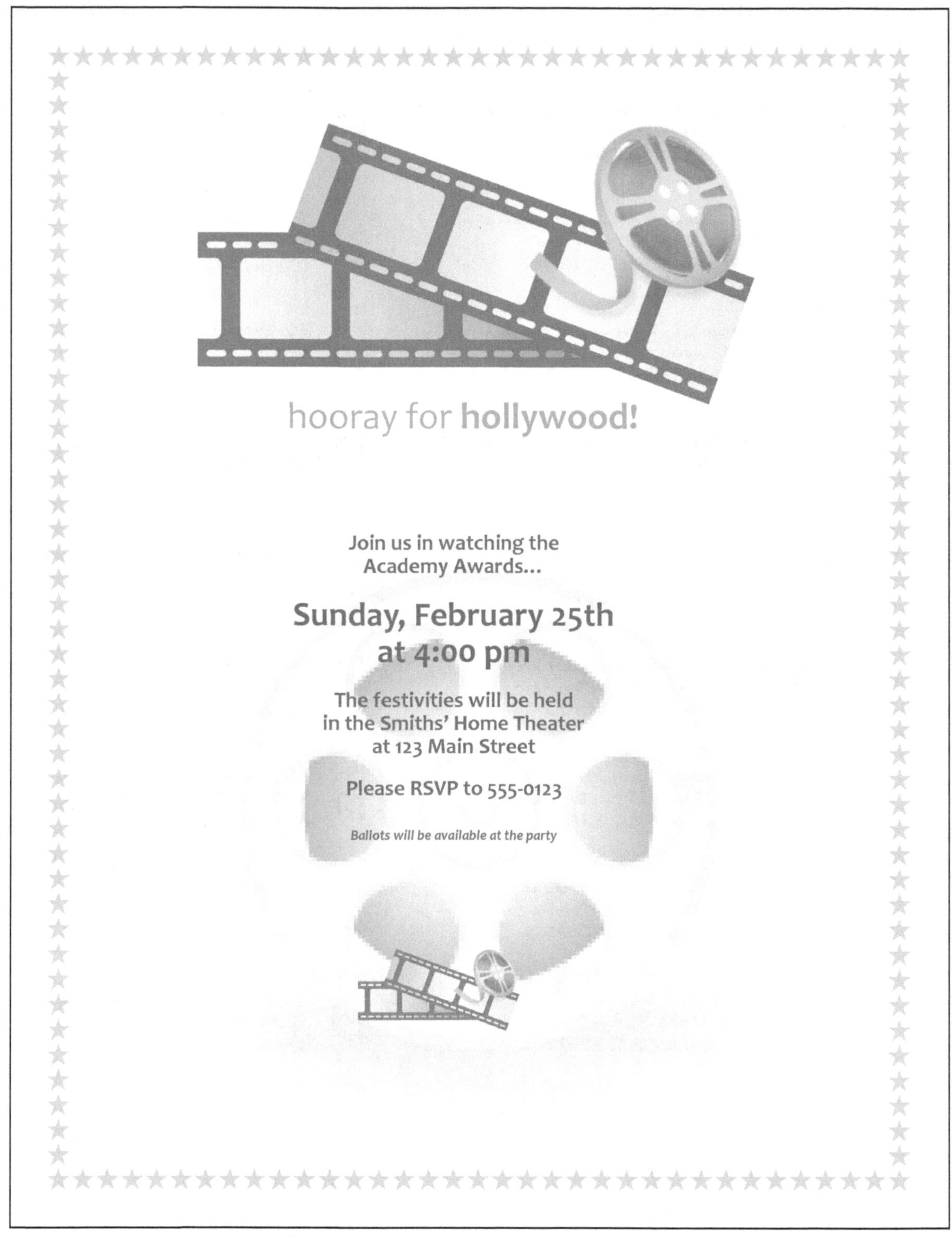

hooray for hollywood!
Join us in watching the
Academy Awards...
Sunday, February 25th
at 4:00 pm
The festivities will be held
in the Smiths' Home Theater
at 123 Main Street
Please RSVP to 555-0123
Ballots will be available at the party

3. Insert the **MovieReel.png** movie reel image (using the Pictures button) with the following specifications:
   - Size the image so it appears as shown in the figure and change the position of the image so it is at the bottom center of the page.
   - Change the text wrapping to behind the text.
4. Make any other changes so your document is similar to Figure WB-6.4.
5. Save the invitation and name it **6-MovieInvite**.
6. Save the invitation document in PDF format with the same name.
7. Open the **6-MovieInvite.pdf** file in Adobe Acrobat Reader, print the file, and then close Adobe Acrobat Reader.
8. Save and then close **6-MovieInvite.docx**.

Case Study

Part 1

You are the office manager for a real estate company, Macadam Realty, and have been asked by the senior sales associate, Lucy Hendricks, to organize contract forms into a specific folder. Create a new folder named *RealEstate* and then copy into it documents that begin with the letters *RE*. Ms. Hendricks has also asked you to prepare mailing labels for Macadam Realty. Include on the labels the name, Macadam Realty, and the address, 100 Third Street, Suite 210, Denver, CO 80803. Use a decorative font for the name and address and make the *M* in *Macadam* and the *R* in *Realty* larger and more pronounced than the surrounding text. Save the completed document and name it **6-RELabels**. Print and then close the document.

Part 2

Data Files

One of your responsibilities at Macadam Realty is to format contract forms. Open **REConAgrmnt.docx** and then save it with the name **6-REConAgrmnt**. Ms. Hendricks has asked you to insert signature information at the end of the document and so you decide to insert the file named **RESig.docx**. With **6-REConAgrmnt.docx** still open, open **REBuildAgrmnt.docx**. Format **6-REConAgrmnt.docx** so it is formatted in a manner similar to **REBuildAgrmnt.docx**. Consider the following when specifying formatting: fonts, font sizes, and paragraph shading. Save, print, and then close **6-REConAgrmnt.docx**. Close **REBuildAgrmnt.docx**.

Part 3

As part of the organization of contracts, Ms. Hendricks has asked you to insert document properties in **REBuildAgrmnt.docx** and **6-REConAgrmnt.docx**. Use the Help feature to learn how to insert document properties. With the information you learn from the Help feature, open each document separately, display the Info backstage area, click the Show All Properties hyperlink (you may need to scroll down the backstage area to display this hyperlink), and then insert document properties in the following fields (you determine the information to type): *Title*, *Categories*, *Subject*, and *Company*. Print the document properties for each document. (Change the first gallery in the *Settings* category in the Print backstage area to *Document Info*.) Save each document with the original name and close the documents.

Part 4

A client of the real estate company, Anna Hurley, is considering purchasing several rental properties and has asked for information on how to locate real estate rental forms. Using the Internet, locate at least three websites that offer real estate rental forms. Write a letter to Anna Hurley at 2300 South 22nd Street, Denver, CO 80205. In the letter, list the websites you found and include information on which site you thought offers the most resources. Also include in the letter that Macadam Realty is very interested in helping her locate and purchase rental properties. Save the document and name it **6-RELtr**. Create an envelope for the letter and add it to the letter document. Save, print, and then close **6-RELtr.docx**. (You may need to manually feed the envelope in the printer.)

Microsoft® Word

Creating Tables and SmartArt

CHAPTER 7

Study Tools

Study tools include a presentation and a list of chapter Quick Steps and Hint margin notes. Use these resources to help you further develop and review skills learned in this chapter.

Concepts Check

Check your understanding by identifying application tools used in this chapter. If you are a SNAP user, launch the Concepts Check from your Assignments page.

Recheck

Check your understanding by taking this quiz. If you are a SNAP user, launch the Recheck from your Assignments page.

Skills Exercise

Additional activities are available to SNAP users. If you are a SNAP user, access these activities from your Assignments page.

Skills Assessment

Assessment 1

Create, Format, and Modify a Training Schedule Table

1. At a blank document, create a table with four columns and five rows.
2. Type text in the cells as shown in Figure WB-7.1.
3. Insert a new column at the right side of the table and then type the following text in the new cells:

   Trainer
   Marsden
   Trujillo
   Yong
   Stein

4. Change the widths of the columns to the following measurements:

   First column = 0.8 inch
   Second column = 1.2 inches
   Third column = 0.7 inch
   Fourth column = 1.3 inches
   Fifth column = 0.9 inch

5. Insert a new row above the first row and then, with the new row selected, merge the cells. Type APPLICATION TRAINING SCHEDULE in the cell and then center the text.
6. Select the second row (contains the text *Section*, *Training*, *Days*, and so on) and then apply bold formatting to and center-align the text.
7. Display the Table Tools Design tab, apply the Grid Table 4 table style (first column, fourth row in the *Grid Tables* section), and then remove the check mark from the *First Column* check box.

Figure WB-7.1 Assessment 1

Section	Training	Days	Time
WD100	Word Level 1	MWF	9:00 to 10:00 a.m.
WD110	Word Level 2	TTh	1:30 to 3:00 p.m.
EX100	Excel Level 1	MTW	3:00 to 4:00 p.m.
EX110	Excel Level 2	TTh	2:00 to 3:30 p.m.

8. Horizontally center the table on the page. ***Hint: Do this at the Table Properties dialog box with the Table tab selected.***
9. Save the document and name it **7-SchTable**.
10. Print and then close **7-SchTable.docx**.

Assessment 2 Create, Format, and Modify a Property Replacement Costs Table

1. At a blank document, create a table with two columns and six rows.
2. Type the text in the cells in the table as shown in Figure WB-7.2. (Press the Enter key after typing the word *PROPERTY* in the first cell.)
3. Merge the cells in the top row and then center-align the text in the merged cell.
4. Right-align the text in the cells containing money amounts and the blank cell below the last amount (cells B2 through B6).
5. Click in the *Accounts receivable* cell and then insert a row below it. Type Equipment in the new cell at the left and type $83,560 in the new cell at the right.
6. Insert a formula in cell B7 that sums the amounts in cells B2 through B6 and then change the number format to *#,##0*. Type a dollar symbol ($) before the amount in cell B7.
7. Automatically fit the contents of the cells.
8. Apply the Grid Table 4 - Accent 1 table style (second column, fourth row in the *Grid Tables* section) and remove the check mark from the *First Column* check box.
9. Click the Border Styles button arrow, click the *Double solid lines, 1/2 pt* option (first column, third row in the *Theme Borders* section), and then draw a border around all four sides of the table.
10. Save the document and name it **7-CostsTable**.
11. Print and then close **7-CostsTable.docx**.

Figure WB-7.2 Assessment 2

PROPERTY REPLACEMENT COSTS	
Accounts receivable	$95,460
Business personal property	$1,367,340
Legal liability	$75,415
Earnings and expenses	$945,235
Total	

Assessment 3

Data Files

Format a Table on Transportation Services

1. Open **ServicesTable.docx** and then save it with the name **7-ServicesTable**.
2. Insert a new column at the left of the table and then merge the cells. Type Metro Area in the merged cell, press the Enter key, and then type Transportation Services.
3. Select the text in the first column, change the font size to 16 points, and then click the Text Direction button two times to rotate the text. ***Hint: The Text Direction button is in the Alignment group on the Table Tools Layout tab.***
4. Center-align (using the Align Center button) the text in the first column.
5. Change the width of the first column to 0.9 inch and the width of the third column to 1.1 inches.
6. Apply the Grid Table 5 Dark - Accent 5 table style (sixth column, fifth row in the *Grid Tables* section).
7. Horizontally center the table on the page.
8. Indent the text in the three cells below the cell containing the text *Valley Railroad,* as shown in Figure WB-7.3.
9. Apply italic and bold formatting to the four headings in the second column (*Langley City Transit*, *Valley Railroad*, *Mainline Bus*, and *Village Travel Card*).
10. Save, print, and then close **7-ServicesTable.docx**.

Figure WB-7.3 Assessment 3

Metro Area Transportation Services	Service	Telephone
	Langley City Transit	
	Subway and bus information	(507) 555-3049
	Service status hotline	(507) 555-4123
	Travel information	(507) 555-4993
	Valley Railroad	
	Railway information	(202) 555-2300
	Status hotline	(202) 555-2343
	Travel information	(202) 555-2132
	Mainline Bus	
	Bus routes	(507) 555-6530
	Emergency hotline	(507) 555-6798
	Travel information	(507) 555-7542
	Village Travel Card	
	Village office	(507) 555-1232
	Card inquiries	(507) 555-1930

Assessment 4

Create and Format a Company SmartArt Graphic

1. At a blank document, create the SmartArt graphic shown in Figure WB-7.4 with the following specifications:
   a. Use the Titled Matrix SmartArt graphic (second option in the *Matrix* section).
   b. Apply the Colorful - Accent Colors SmartArt style (first option in the *Colorful* section).
   c. Apply the Polished SmartArt style (first column, first row in the *3-D* section).

d. With the middle shape selected, apply the Intense Effect - Green, Accent 6 shape style. (Click the SmartArt Tools Format tab, click the More Shape Styles button in the gallery in the Shape Styles group and then click the last option in the *Theme Styles* section.)
e. Type all of the text shown in Figure WB-7.4.
f. Select only the SmartArt graphic (not a specific shape) and then apply the Fill - Black, Text 1, Outline - Background 1, Hard Shadow - Background 1 WordArt style (first column, third row) to the text.
g. Change the height of the SmartArt graphic to 3.2 inches and the width to 5.3 inches.
h. Position the SmartArt graphic at the top center of the page with square text wrapping.

2. Save the document and name it **7-OCGraphic**.
3. Print and then close **7-OCGraphic.docx**.

Figure WB-7.4 Assessment 4

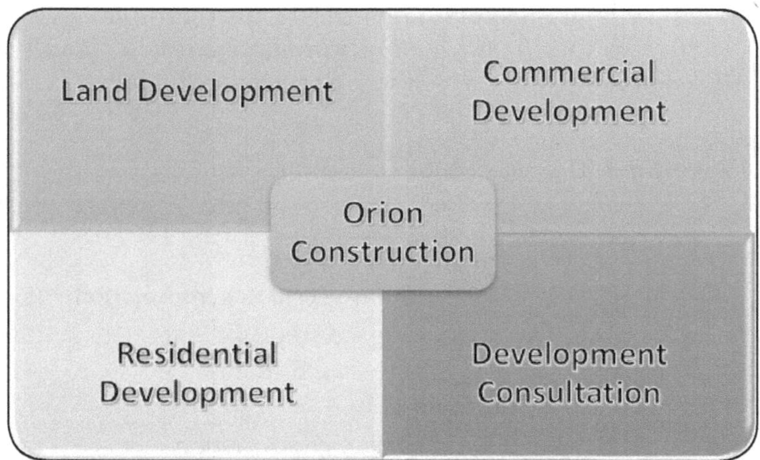

Assessment 5

Create and Format a Company Organizational Chart

1. At a blank document, create the organizational chart shown in Figure WB-7.5 with the following specifications:
   a. Use the Hierarchy SmartArt graphic (second column, second row with *Hierarchy* selected in the left panel).
   b. With the top text box selected, add a shape above it.
   c. Select the text box at the right in the third row and then add a shape below it.
   d. Type the text shown in the organizational chart in Figure WB-7.5.
   e. Apply the Colorful Range - Accent Colors 3 to 4 SmartArt style (third option in the *Colorful* section).
   f. Increase the height to 4.5 inches and the width to 6.5 inches.
   g. Position the organizational chart in the middle of the page with square text wrapping.
2. Save the document and name it **7-CoOrgChart**.
3. Print and then close **7-CoOrgChart.docx**.

Figure WB-7.5 Assessment 5

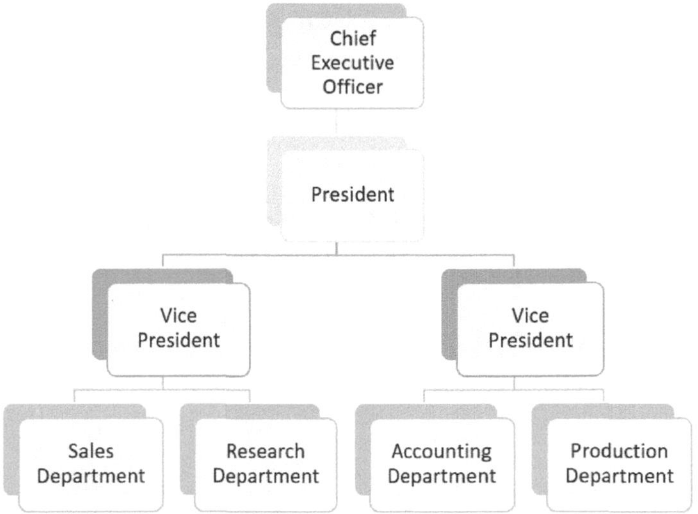

Assessment 6

Data Files

Insert Formulas in a Table

1. In this chapter, you learned how to insert formulas in a table. Experiment with writing formulas (consider using the Help feature or another reference) and then open **FinAnalysis.docx**. Save the document and name it **7-FinAnalysis**.
2. Apply the Grid Table 4 - Accent 6 table style to the table and then apply other formatting so your table appears similar to the one in Figure WB-7.6.
3. Insert a formula in cell B13 that sums the amounts in cells B6 through B12. Apply the #,##0 format. Type a dollar symbol ($) before the amount. Complete similar steps to insert formulas and dollar symbols in cells C13, D13, and E13.
4. Insert a formula in cell B14 that subtracts the amount in B13 from the amount in B4. Apply the #,##0 format. ***Hint: The formula should look like this:*** **=(B4-B13)**. Type a dollar symbol before the amount. Complete similar steps to insert formulas and dollar symbols in cells C14, D14, and E14.
5. Save, print, and then close **7-FinAnalysis.docx**.

Figure WB-7.6 Assessment 6

TRI-STATE PRODUCTS				
Financial Analysis				
	2015	**2016**	**2017**	**2018**
Revenue	$1,450,348	$1,538,239	$1,634,235	$1,523,455
Expenses				
Facilities	$250,220	$323,780	$312,485	$322,655
Materials	$93,235	$102,390	$87,340	$115,320
Payroll	$354,390	$374,280	$380,120	$365,120
Benefits	$32,340	$35,039	$37,345	$36,545
Marketing	$29,575	$28,350	$30,310	$31,800
Transportation	$4,492	$5,489	$5,129	$6,349
Miscellaneous	$4,075	$3,976	$4,788	$5,120
Total				
Net Revenue				

Visual Benchmark

Part 1

Create a Cover Letter Containing a Table

1. Click the File tab, click the *New* option, and then double-click the *Single spaced (blank)* template.
2. At the single-spaced blank document, type the letter shown in Figure WB-7.7. Create and format the table in the letter as shown in the figure. ***Hint: Apply the Grid Table 4 - Accent 1 table style.***
3. Save the completed document and name it **7-CoverLtr**.
4. Print and then close **7-CoverLtr.docx**.

Figure WB-7.7 Visual Benchmark 1

10234 Larkspur Drive *(press Enter)*
Cheyenne, WY 82002 *(press Enter)*
July 15, 2018 *(press Enter five times)*

Dr. Theresa Sullivan *(press Enter)*
Rocky Mountain News *(press Enter)*
100 Second Avenue *(press Enter)*
Cheyenne, WY 82001 *(press Enter two times)*

Dear Dr. Sullivan: *(press Enter two times)*

Your advertised opening for a corporate communications staff writer describes interesting challenges. As you can see from the table below, my skills and experience are excellent matches for the position.

QUALIFICATIONS AND SKILLS	
Your Requirement	**My Experience, Skills, and Value Offered**
Two years of business writing experience	Four years of experience creating diverse business messages, from corporate communications to feature articles and radio broadcast material.
Ability to complete projects on deadline	Proven project coordination skills and tight deadline focus. My current role as producer of a daily three-hour talk-radio program requires planning, coordination, and execution of many detailed tasks, always in the face of inflexible deadlines.
Oral presentation skills	Unusually broad experience, including high-profile roles as an on-air radio presence and "the voice" for an on-hold telephone message company.
Relevant education (BA or BS)	BA in Mass Communications; one year post-graduate study in Multimedia Communications.

As you will note from the enclosed résumé, my experience encompasses corporate, print media, and multimedia environments. I offer a diverse and proven skill set that can help your company create and deliver its message to various audiences to build image, market presence, and revenue. I look forward to meeting with you to discuss the value I can offer your company. *(press Enter two times)*

Sincerely, *(press Enter four times)*

Marcus Tolliver *(press Enter two times)*

Enclosure: Résumé

Part 2

Create and Format a SmartArt Graphic

1. At a blank document, create the document shown in Figure WB-7.8. Create and format the SmartArt graphic as shown in the figure. ***Hint: Use the Step Up Process graphic.*** Change the width of the SmartArt graphic to 6.5 inches.
2. Save the completed document and name it **7-SalesGraphic**.
3. Print and then close **7-SalesGraphic.docx**.

Figure WB-7.8 Visual Benchmark 2

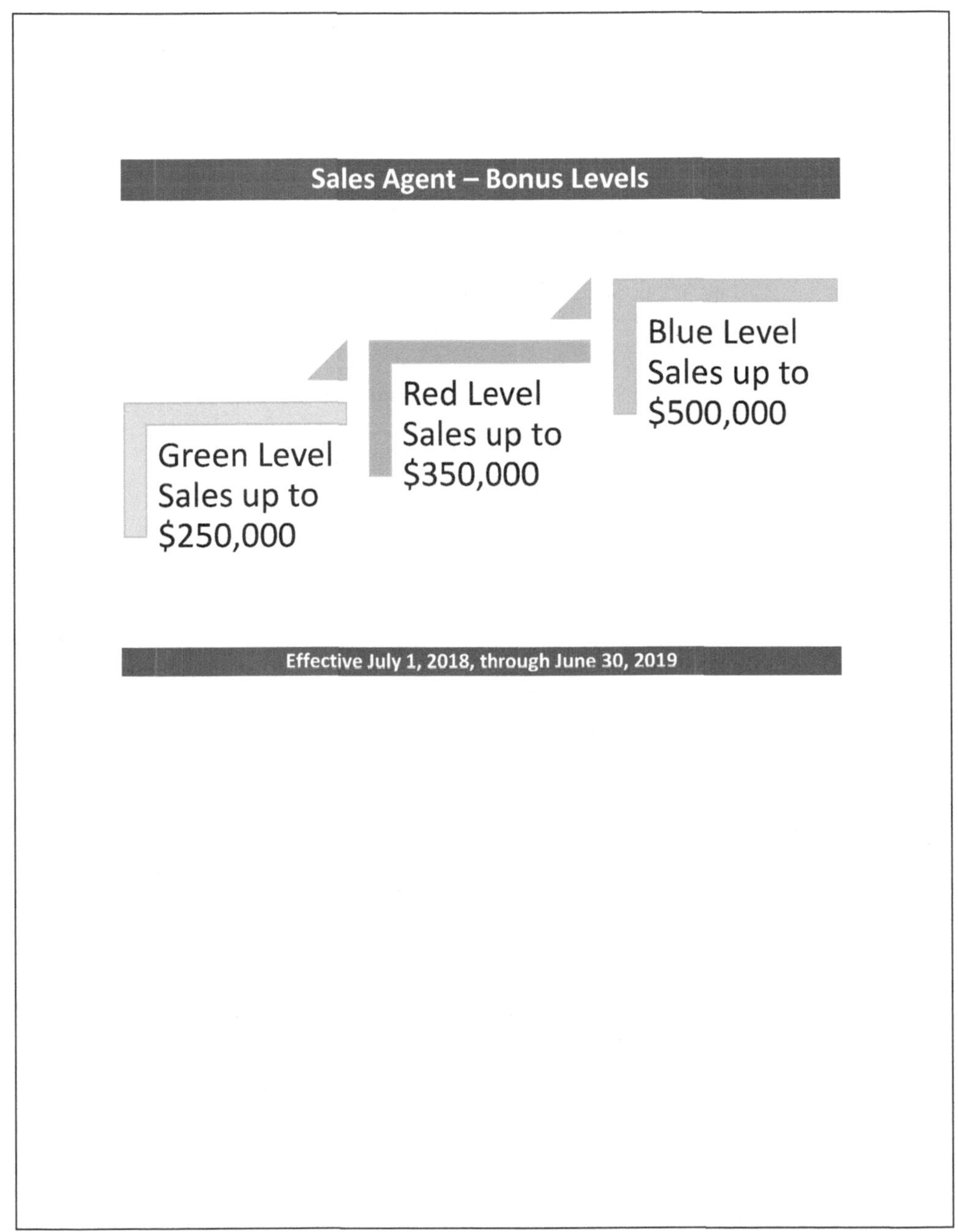

Case Study

Part 1

Data Files

You have recently been hired as an accounting clerk for a landscaping business, Landmark Landscaping, which has two small offices in your city. The person who held the position before kept track of monthly sales using Word and the company manager would prefer that you continue using that application. Open the file named **LLMoSales.docx** and then save it with the name **7-LLMoSales**. After reviewing the information, you decide that a table would be a better format for maintaining and displaying the data. Convert the data to a table and modify its appearance so that it is easy to read and understand. Insert a *Total* row at the bottom of the table and then insert formulas to sum the totals in the columns that contain amounts. Apply formatting to the table to enhance its appearance. Determine a color theme for the table and then continue to use that color theme when preparing other documents for Landmark Landscaping. Save, print, and then close the document.

Part 2

The president of Landmark Landscaping has asked you to prepare an organizational chart that will become part of the company profile. Create a SmartArt organizational chart using the position titles shown in Figure WB-7.9. Use the order and structure in Figure WB-7.9 to guide the layout of the SmartArt chart.

Format the organizational chart to enhance its appearance and apply colors that match the color scheme you chose in Part 1. Save the document and name it **7-LLOrgChart**. Print and then close the document.

Figure WB-7.9 Case Study, Part 2

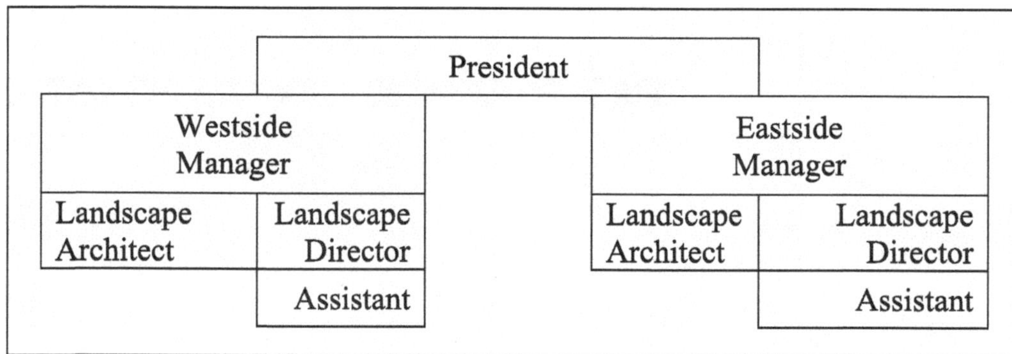

Part 3

As part of the company profile, the president of Landmark Landscaping would like to include a graphic that represents the services the company offers and use the graphic as a marketing tool. Use SmartArt to create a graphic that contains the following services: Maintenance Contracts, Planting Services, Landscape Design, and Landscape Consultation. Format the SmartArt graphic to enhance its appearance and apply colors that match the color scheme you chose in Part 1. Save the document and name it **7-LLServices**. Print and then close the document.

Part 4

The office manager of Landmark Landscaping has started to create a training document on using SmartArt. He has asked you to add information on keyboard shortcuts for working with shapes in a SmartArt graphic. Use the Help feature to learn about the keyboard shortcuts available for working with shapes and then create a table and insert the information in it. Format the table to enhance its appearance and apply colors that match the color scheme you chose in Part 1. Save the document and name it **7-SAShortcuts**. Print and then close the document.

Part 5

One of the landscape architects at Landmark Landscaping has asked you to prepare a table containing information on the trees that need to be ordered next month. She would also like you to include the Latin names for the trees, because this information is important when ordering. Create a table that contains the common name of each tree, the Latin name, quantity required, and the price per tree, as shown in Figure WB-7.10. Use the Internet (or any other resource available to you) to find the Latin name of each tree listed in Figure WB-7.10. Create a column in the table that multiplies the number of trees to be ordered by the price and include this formula for each tree. Format and enhance the table so it is attractive and easy to read and apply colors that match the color scheme you chose in Part 1. Save the document and name it **7-LLTrees**. Print and then close the document.

Figure WB-7.10 Case Study, Part 5

Douglas Fir, 15 required, $1.99 per tree
Elm, 10 required, $2.49 per tree
Western Hemlock, 10 required, $1.89 per tree
Red Maple, 8 required, $6.99 per tree
Ponderosa Pine, 5 required, $2.69 per tree

Merging Documents

Study Tools

Study tools include a presentation and a list of chapter Quick Steps and Hint margin notes. Use these resources to help you further develop and review skills learned in this chapter.

Concepts Check

Check your understanding by identifying application tools used in this chapter. If you are a SNAP user, launch the Concepts Check from your Assignments page.

Recheck

Check your understanding by taking this quiz. If you are a SNAP user, launch the Recheck from your Assignments page.

Skills Exercise

Additional activities are available to SNAP users. If you are a SNAP user, access these activities from your Assignments page.

Skills Assessment

Assessment 1

Create a Data Source File

1. At a blank document, display the New Address List dialog box and then display the Customize Address List dialog box.
2. At the Customize Address List dialog box, delete the following fields—*Company Name*, *Country or Region*, *Work Phone*, and *E-mail Address*—and then add a custom field named *Cell Phone*.
3. Close the Customize Address List box and then type the following information in the New Address List dialog box as the first record:

Title	Mr.
First Name	Tony
Last Name	Benedetti
Address Line 1	1315 Cordova Road
Address Line 2	Apt. 402
City	Santa Fe
State	NM
ZIP Code	87505
Home Phone	(505) 555-0489
Cell Phone	(505) 555-0551

4. Type the following information as the second record:

Title	Ms.
First Name	Theresa
Last Name	Dusek
Address Line 1	12044 Ridgeway Drive

Address Line 2	(leave blank)
City	Santa Fe
State	NM
ZIP Code	87504
Home Phone	(505) 555-1120
Cell Phone	(505) 555-6890

5. Type the following information as the third record:

Title	Mrs.
First Name	Mary
Last Name	Arguello
Address Line 1	2554 Country Drive
Address Line 2	#105
City	Santa Fe
State	NM
ZIP Code	87504
Home Phone	(505) 555-7663
Cell Phone	(505) 555-5472

6. Type the following information as the fourth record:

Title	Mr.
First Name	Preston
Last Name	Miller
Address Line 1	120 Second Street
Address Line 2	(leave blank)
City	Santa Fe
State	NM
ZIP Code	87505
Home Phone	(505) 555-3551
Cell Phone	(505) 555-9630

7. Save the data source file and name it **8-CCDS**.
8. Close the blank document without saving changes.

Assessment 2

Data Files

Create a Main Document and Merge with a Data Source File

1. Open **CCVolunteerLtr.docx** and then save it with the name **8-CCMD**.
2. Select **8-CCDS.mdb**, which you created in Assessment 1, as the data source file.
3. Move the insertion point to the beginning of the first paragraph of text in the body of the letter, insert the «AddressBlock» field, and then press the Enter key two times.
4. Insert the «GreetingLine» field specifying a colon rather than a comma as the greeting line format and then press the Enter key two times.
5. Move the insertion point one space to the right of the period that ends the second paragraph of text in the body of the letter and then type the following text inserting the «Title», «Last_Name», «Home_Phone», «Cell_Phone» fields where indicated:

   Currently, «Title» «Last_Name», our records indicate your home telephone number is «Home_Phone» and your cell phone number is «Cell_Phone». If this information is not accurate, please contact our office with the correct numbers.

6. Merge the main document with all the records in the data source file.
7. Save the merged letters document as **8-CCLetters**.
8. Print and then close **8-CCLetters.docx**.
9. Save and then close **8-CCMD.docx**.

Assessment 3 Create an Envelope Main Document and Merge with a Data Source File

1. Create an envelope main document using the Size 10 envelope size.
2. Select **8-CCDS.mdb** as the data source file.
3. Insert the «AddressBlock» field in the appropriate location in the envelope document.
4. Merge the envelope main document with all the records in the data source file.
5. Save the merged envelopes document and name it **8-CCEnvs**.
6. Print and then close the envelopes document. (Check with your instructor before printing the envelopes.)
7. Close the envelope main document without saving it.

Assessment 4 Create a Labels Main Document and Merge with a Data Source File

1. Create a labels main document using the option *Avery US Letter 5160 Easy Peel Address Labels*.
2. Select **8-CCDS.mdb** as the data source file.
3. Insert the «AddressBlock» field.
4. Update the labels.
5. Merge the labels main document with all the records in the data source file.
6. Select the entire document and then apply the No Spacing style.
7. Save the merged labels document and name it **8-CCLabels**.
8. Print and then close the labels document.
9. Close the labels main document without saving it.

Assessment 5 Edit a Data Source File

1. Open **8-CCMD.docx**. (At the message asking if you want to continue, click Yes.) Save the main document with the name **8-CCMD-A5**.
2. Edit the **8-CCDS.mdb** data source file by making the following changes:
   a. Change the address for Ms. Theresa Dusek from *12044 Ridgeway Drive* to *1390 Fourth Avenue*.
   b. Delete the record for Mrs. Mary Arguello.
   c. Insert a new record with the following information:
      Mr. Cesar Rivera
      3201 East Third Street
      Santa Fe, NM 87505
      Home Phone: (505) 555-6675
      Cell Phone: (505) 555-3528
3. At the main document, edit the third sentence of the second paragraph so it reads as follows (insert a fill-in field for the *(number of hours)* shown in the sentence below):
   According to our volunteer roster, you have signed up to volunteer for *(number of hours)* during the summer session.
4. Merge the main document with the data source file and type the following text for each record:
   Record 1: four hours a week
   Record 2: six hours a week
   Record 3: twelve hours a week
   Record 4: four hours a week
5. Save the merged document and name it **8-CCLtrs_Fill-in**.
6. Print and then close **8-CCLtrs_Fill-in.docx**.
7. Save and then close **8-CCMD-A5.docx**.

Visual Benchmark

Prepare and Merge Letters

Data Files

1. Open **FPLtrhd.docx** and then save it with the name **8-FPMD**.
2. Look at the information in Figure WB-8.1 and Figure WB-8.2 and then use Mail Merge to prepare four letters. (When creating the main document, as shown in Figure WB-8.2, insert the appropriate fields where you see the text *Title*; *First Name*; *Last Name*; *Street Address*; and *City, State ZIP*. Insert the appropriate fields where you see the text *Title* and *Last Name* in the greeting line and in the first paragraph of text.) Create the data source file, with customized field names, with the information in Figure WB-8.1 and then save the file and name it **8-FPDS**.
3. Merge the **8-FPMD.docx** main document with the **8-FPDS.mdb** data source file and then save the merged letters document and name it **8-FPLtrs**.
4. Print and then close **8-FPLtrs.docx**.
5. Save and then close **8-FPMD.docx**.

Figure WB-8.1 Visual Benchmark Data Source Records

Mr. Chris Gallagher
17034 234th Avenue
Newport, VT 05855

Ms. Heather Segarra
4103 Thompson Drive
Newport, VT 05855

Mr. Gene Goodrich
831 Cromwell Lane
Newport, VT 05855

Mrs. Sonya Kraus
15933 Ninth Street
Newport, VT 05855

Figure WB-8.2 Visual Benchmark Main Document

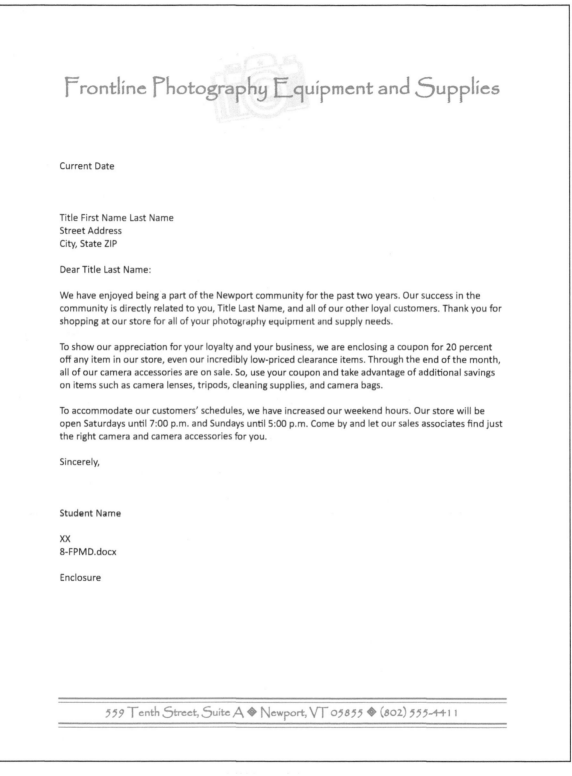

Frontline Photography Equipment and Supplies

Current Date

Title First Name Last Name
Street Address
City, State ZIP

Dear Title Last Name:

We have enjoyed being a part of the Newport community for the past two years. Our success in the community is directly related to you, Title Last Name, and all of our other loyal customers. Thank you for shopping at our store for all of your photography equipment and supply needs.

To show our appreciation for your loyalty and your business, we are enclosing a coupon for 20 percent off any item in our store, even our incredibly low-priced clearance items. Through the end of the month, all of our camera accessories are on sale. So, use your coupon and take advantage of additional savings on items such as camera lenses, tripods, cleaning supplies, and camera bags.

To accommodate our customers' schedules, we have increased our weekend hours. Our store will be open Saturdays until 7:00 p.m. and Sundays until 5:00 p.m. Come by and let our sales associates find just the right camera and camera accessories for you.

Sincerely,

Student Name

XX
8-FPMD.docx

Enclosure

559 Tenth Street, Suite A ◈ Newport, VT 05855 ◈ (802) 555-4411

Case Study

Part 1

You are the office manager for Freestyle Extreme, a sporting goods store that specializes in snowboarding and snow skiing equipment and supplies. The store has two branches: one on the east side of town and the other on the west side. One of your job responsibilities is to send letters to customers letting them know about sales, new equipment, and upcoming events. Next month, both stores are having a sale and all snowboard and snow skiing supplies will be 15 percent off the regular price. Create a data source file that contains the following customer information: first name, last name, address, city, state, zip code, and branch. Add six customers to the data source file. Indicate that three usually shop at the East branch and three usually shop at the West branch. Create a letter as a main document that includes information about the upcoming sale. The letter should contain at least two paragraphs and in addition to the information on the sale, it might include information about the store, snowboarding, and/or snow skiing. Save the data source file with the name **8-FEDS**, save the main document with the name **8-FEMD**, and save the merged document with the name **8-FELtrs**. Create envelopes for the six merged letters and name the merged envelope document **8-FEEnvs**. Do not save the envelope main document. Print the merged letters document and the merged envelopes document.

Part 2

A well-known extreme snowboarder will be visiting both branches of Freestyle Extreme to meet with customers and sign autographs. Use the Help feature to learn how to insert an *If...Then...Else...* merge field in a document, and then create a letter that includes the name of the extreme snowboarder (you determine the name), the time of the visits (1:00 p.m. to 4:30 p.m.), and any additional information that might interest customers. Also include in the letter an *If... Then...Else...* merge field that will insert *Wednesday, September 26* if the customer's branch is *East* and will insert *Thursday, September 27* if the branch is *West*. Add visual appeal to the letter by inserting an image, WordArt, or any other feature that will attract readers' attention. Save the letter main document and name it **8-SnowMD**. Merge the letter main document with the **8-FEDS.mdb** data source file. Save the merged letters document and name it **8-SnowLtrs**. Print the merged letters document.

Part 3

The owner of Freestyle Extreme wants to try selling short skis known as "snow blades" or "skiboards." He has asked you to research these skis and identify one type and model to sell only at the West branch of the store. If the model sells well, the owner will consider selling it at the East branch at a future time. Prepare a main document letter that describes the new snow blade or skiboard that the West branch is going to sell. Include information about pricing and tell customers that they can save 40 percent if they purchase the new item within the next week. Merge the letter main document with the **8-FEDS.mdb** data source file and include only those customers that shop at the West branch. Save the merged letters document and name it **8-SBLtrs**. Print the merged letters document. Save the letter main document and name it **8-SBMD**. Save and then close the main document.

Microsoft®

Word Level 1

Unit 2 Performance Assessment

Data Files

Before beginning unit work, copy the WL1U2 folder to your storage medium and then make WL1U2 the active folder.

Assessing Proficiency

In this unit, you have learned to format text into columns; insert, format, and customize objects to enhance the appearance of documents; manage files, print envelopes and labels, and create documents using templates; create and edit tables; visually represent data in SmartArt graphics and organizational charts; and use Mail Merge to create letters, envelopes, labels, and directories.

Assessment 1

Data Files

Format a Bioinformatics Document

1. Open **Bioinformatics.docx** and then save it with the name **U2-Bioinformatics**.
2. Move the insertion point to the end of the document and then insert the file named **GenomeMapping.docx**.
3. Change the line spacing for the entire document to 1.5 spacing.
4. Insert a continuous section break at the beginning of the first paragraph of text (the paragraph that begins *Bioinformatics is the mixed application*).
5. Format the text below the section break into two columns.
6. Balance the columns on the second page.
7. Press Ctrl + Home to move the insertion point to the beginning of the document, insert the Motion Quote text box, and then type "Understanding our DNA is similar to understanding a number that is billions of digits long." in the text box. Select the text in the text box, change the font size to 12 points, change the width of the text box to 2.6 inches, and then position the text box in the middle of the page and apply square text wrapping.
8. Create a drop cap with the first letter of the first word *Bioinformatics* that begins the first paragraph of text. Make the drop cap two lines in height.
9. Manually hyphenate the words in the document.
10. Insert page numbering at the bottom of the page using the Thin Line page numbering option.
11. Save, print, and then close **U2-Bioinformatics.docx**.

Assessment 2

Data Files

Create a Workshop Flyer

1. Create the flyer shown in Figure WB-U2.1 with the following specifications:
   a. Create the WordArt with the following specifications:
      - Use the *Fill - White, Outline - Accent 1, Shadow* option (fourth column, first row) at the WordArt button drop-down gallery.
      - Increase the width to 6.5 inches and the height to 1 inch.
      - Apply the Deflate text effect transform shape (second column, sixth row in the *Warp* section).
      - Position the WordArt in the top center of the page and apply square text wrapping.
      - Change the text fill color to Green, Accent 6, Lighter 40% (last column, fourth row in the *Theme Colors* section).

   b. Type the text shown in the figure. Change the font to 22-point Calibri, apply bold formatting, and center-align the text.
   c. Insert the **EiffelTower.png** image. Change the wrapping style to Square and size and position the image as shown in Figure WB-U2.1.
2. Save the document and name it **U2-TravelFlyer**.
3. Print and then close **U2-TravelFlyer.docx**.

Figure WB-U2.1 Assessment 2

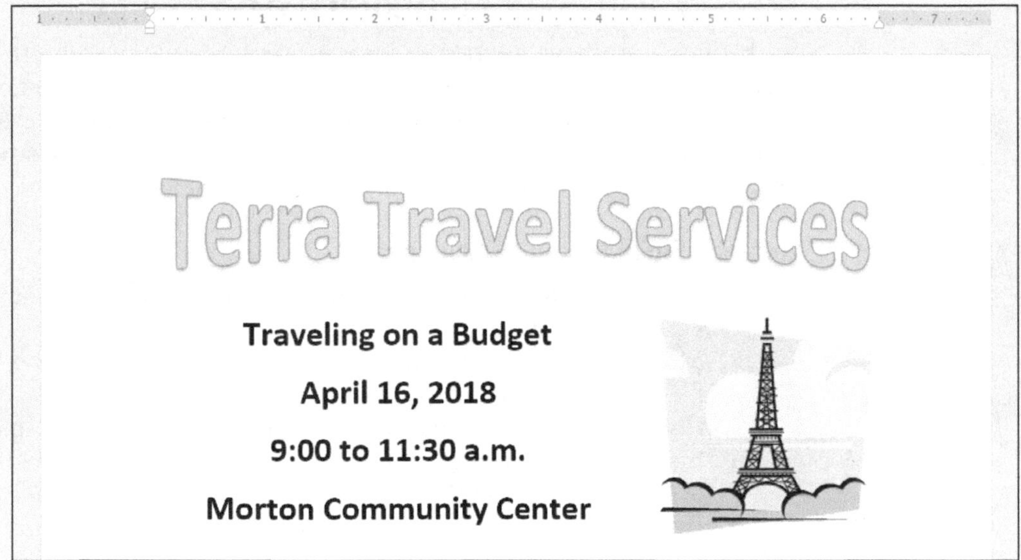

Assessment 3

Create a Staff Meeting Announcement

1. Create the announcement shown in Figure WB-U2.2 with the following specifications:
   a. Use the Hexagon shape in the *Basic Shapes* section of the Shapes button drop-down list to create the shape.
   b. Apply the Subtle Effect - Blue, Accent 1 shape style (second column, fourth row in the *Theme Styles* section).
   c. Apply the Art Deco bevel shape effect (last option in the *Bevel* section).
   d. Type the letter A (this makes active many of the tab options), click the Home tab, and then click the *No Spacing* style in the styles gallery.

e. Type the remaining text in the shape as shown in Figure WB-U2.2. Insert the *ñ* as a symbol (in the normal text font) and insert the clock as a symbol (in the Wingdings font, character code 185). Set the text and clock symbol in larger font sizes.
2. Save the completed document and name it **U2-MeetNotice**.
3. Print and then close **U2-MeetNotice.docx**.

Figure WB-U2.2 Assessment 3

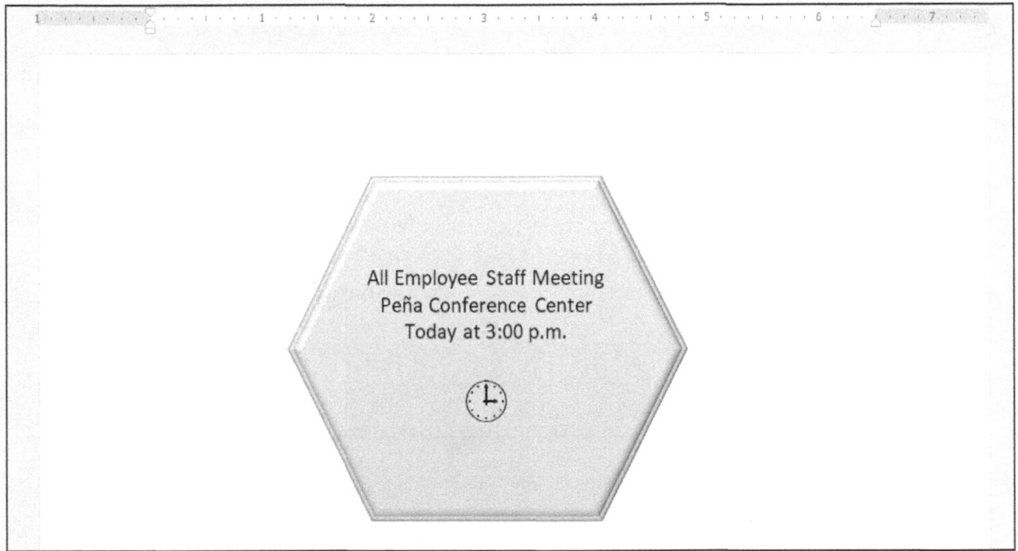

Assessment 4

Data Files

Create a River Rafting Flyer

1. At a blank document, insert the **River.jpg** file.
2. Crop off some of the trees at the left and right and some of the hill at the top.
3. Correct the brightness and contrast to Brightness: +20% Contrast: +40%.
4. Specify that the image should wrap behind text.
5. Type the text River Rafting Adventures on the first line, Salmon River, Idaho on the second line, and 1-888-555-3322 on the third line.
6. Increase the size of the image so it is easier to see and the size of the text so it is easier to read. Center and bold the text and to make it more readable, position it on the image above the river.
7. Save the document and name it **U2-RaftingFlyer**.
8. Print and then close **U2-RaftingFlyer.docx**.

Assessment 5 Create an Envelope

1. At a blank document, create an envelope with the text shown in Figure WB-U2.3.
2. Save the envelope document and name it **U2-Env**.
3. Print and then close **U2-Env.docx**.

Figure WB-U2.3 Assessment 5

Mrs. Eileen Hebert
15205 East 42nd Street
Lake Charles, LA 71098

Mr. Earl Robicheaux
1436 North Sheldon Street
Jennings, LA 70542

Assessment 6 Create Mailing Labels

1. Create mailing labels with the name and address for Mrs. Eileen Hebert shown in Figure WB-U2.3 using a label vendor and product of your choosing.
2. Save the document and name it **U2-Labels**.
3. Print and then close **U2-Labels.docx**.

Assessment 7 Create and Format a Table with Software Training Information

1. At a blank document, create the table shown in Figure WB-U2.4. Format the table and the text (do not apply a table style) in a manner similar to what is shown in Figure WB-U2.4.
2. Insert a formula in cell B8 that totals the numbers in cells B4 through B7.
3. Insert a formula in cell C8 that totals the numbers in cells C4 through C7.
4. Save the document and name it **U2-TechTraining**.
5. Print and then close **U2-TechTraining.docx**.

Figure WB-U2.4 Assessment 7

TRI-STATE PRODUCTS		
Computer Technology Department Microsoft® Office 2016 Training		
Application	# Enrolled	# Completed
Access 2016	20	15
Excel 2016	62	56
PowerPoint 2016	40	33
Word 2016	80	72
Total	202	176

Assessment 8

Data Files

Create and Format a Table Containing Training Scores

1. Open **TrainingScores.docx** and then save it with the name **U2-TrainingScores**.
2. Insert formulas that calculate the averages in the appropriate rows and columns. (When writing the formulas, change the *Number format* option to *0*.)
3. Autofit the contents of the table.
4. Apply a table style of your choosing.
5. Apply any other formatting to improve the appearance of the table.
6. Save, print, and then close **U2-TrainingScores.docx**.

Assessment 9

Create an Organizational Chart

1. Use SmartArt to create an organizational chart for the text shown in Figure WB-U2.5 (in the order displayed). Change the colors to Colorful Range - Accent Colors 4 to 5 and apply the Metallic Scene SmartArt style.
2. Save the completed document and name it **U2-OrgChart**.
3. Print and then close **U2-OrgChart.docx**.

Figure WB-U2.5 Assessment 9

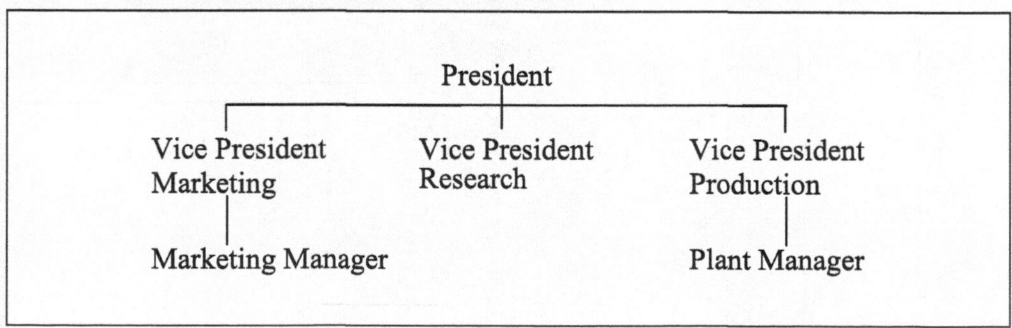

Assessment

10

Data Files

Create a SmartArt Graphic

1. At a blank document, create the WordArt and SmartArt graphic shown in Figure WB-U2.6 with the following specifications:
   a. Create the WordArt text using the *Fill - Blue, Accent 1, Outline - Background 1, Hard Shadow - Accent 1* option. Change the shape height to 1 inch and the shape width to 6 inches and then apply the Square transform text effect. Position the WordArt at the top center of the page and apply square text wrapping.
   b. Create the SmartArt graphic using the Vertical Picture Accent List graphic. Click the picture icon in the top circle and then insert the picture named **Seagull.jpg**. Insert the same picture in the other two circles. Type the text in each rectangle shape as shown in Figure WB-U2.6. Change the colors to *Colorful Range - Accent Colors 5 to 6* and apply the Cartoon SmartArt style.
2. Save the document and name it **U2-SPGraphic**.
3. Print and then close **U2-SPGraphic.docx**.

Figure WB-U2.6 Assessment 10

Assessment 11

Data Files

Merge and Print Letters

1. Look at the information shown in Figure WB-U2.7 and Figure WB-U2.8. Use the Mail Merge feature to prepare six letters using the information shown in the figures. When creating the letter main document, open **SoundLtrhd.docx** and then save it with the name **U2-SoundMD**. Insert the *Title* and *First_Name* fields in the last paragraph as indicated and insert fill-in fields in the main document in place of the *(coordinator name)* and *(telephone number)* text. Create the data source file with the text shown in Figure WB-U2.7 and name the file **U2-SoundDS**.
2. Type the text in the main document as shown in Figure WB-U2.8 and then merge the document with the **U2-SoundDS.mdb** data source file. When merging, enter the first name and telephone number shown below for the first three records and enter the second name and telephone number shown below for the last three records:

   Jeff Greenswald (813) 555-9886
   Grace Ramirez (813) 555-9807
3. Save the merged letters document and name it **U2-SoundLtrs**. Print and then close the document.
4. Save and then close the main document.

Figure WB-U2.7 Assessment 11

Mr. Antonio Mercado
3241 Court G
Tampa, FL 33623

Ms. Kristina Vukovich
1120 South Monroe
Tampa, FL 33655

Ms. Alexandria Remick
909 Wheeler South
Tampa, FL 33620

Mr. Minh Vu
9302 Lawndale Southwest
Tampa, FL 33623

Mr. Curtis Iverson
10139 93rd Court South
Tampa, FL 33654

Mrs. Holly Bernard
8904 Emerson Road
Tampa, FL 33620

Figure WB-U2.8 Assessment 11

December 12, 2018

«AddressBlock»

«GreetingLine»

Sound Medical is switching hospital care in Tampa to St. Jude's Hospital beginning January 1, 2019. As mentioned in last month's letter, St. Jude's Hospital was selected because it meets our requirements for high-quality, customer-pleasing care that is also affordable and accessible. Our physicians look forward to caring for you in this new environment.

Over the past month, staff members at Sound Medical have been working to make this transition as smooth as possible. Surgeries planned after January 1 are being scheduled at St. Jude's Hospital. Mothers delivering babies any time after January 1 are receiving information about delivery room tours and prenatal classes available at St. Jude's. Your Sound Medical doctor will have privileges at St. Jude's and will continue to care for you if you need to be hospitalized.

You are a very important part of our patient family, «Title» «Last_Name», and we hope this information is helpful. If you have any additional questions or concerns, please call your Sound Medical health coordinator, (coordinator name), at (telephone number), between 8:00 a.m. and 4:30 p.m.

Sincerely,

Jody Tiemann
District Administrator

XX
U2-SoundMD.docx

Assessment 12

Merge and Print Envelopes

1. Use the Mail Merge feature to prepare envelopes for the letters created in Assessment 11.
2. Specify **U2-SoundDS.mdb** as the data source document.
3. Save the merged envelopes document and name the document **U2-SoundEnvs**.
4. Print and then close **U2-SoundEnvs.docx**.
5. Do not save the envelope main document.

Writing Activities

The following activities give you the opportunity to practice your writing skills along with demonstrating an understanding of some of the important Word features you have mastered in this unit. Use correct grammar, appropriate word choices, and clear sentence construction.

Activity 1

Compose a Letter to Volunteers

You are an employee of the city of Greenwater and responsible for coordinating volunteers for the city's Safe Night program. Compose a letter to the volunteers listed in Figure WB-U2.9 and include the following information:

- Safe Night event scheduled for Saturday, June 16, 2018.
- Volunteer orientation scheduled for Thursday, May 17, 2018, at 7:30 p.m. At the orientation, participants will learn about the types of volunteer positions available and the corresponding work schedule.

Include additional information in the letter, including a thank you to the volunteers. Use the Mail Merge feature to create a data source with the names and addresses shown in Figure WB-U2.9 that is attached to the main document, which is the letter to the volunteers. Save the merged letters as **U2-VolunteerLtrs** and then print them.

Figure WB-U2.9 Activity 1

Mrs. Laura Reston
376 Thompson Avenue
Greenwater, OR 99034

Mr. Matthew Klein
7408 Ryan Road
Greenwater, OR 99034

Ms. Cecilia Sykes
1430 Canyon Road
Greenwater, OR 99034

Mr. Brian McDonald
8980 Union Street
Greenwater, OR 99034

Mr. Ralph Emerson
1103 Highlands Avenue
Greenwater, OR 99034

Mrs. Nola Alverez
598 McBride Street
Greenwater, OR 99034

Activity 2

Create a Business Letterhead

You have just opened a new mailing and shipping business and need letterhead stationery. Click the Insert tab, click the Header button, and then click *Edit Header* at the drop-down list. Look at the options in the Options group on the Header & Footer Tools Design tab and then figure out how to create a header that displays and prints only on the first page. Create a letterhead for your company in a header that displays and prints only on the first page and include *at least* one of the following: an image, shape, text box, and/or WordArt. Include the following information in the header:

Global Mailing
4300 Jackson Avenue
Toronto, ON M4C 3X4
(416) 555-0095
emcp.net/globalmailing

Save the completed letterhead and name it **U2-GlobalLtrhd**. Print and then close the document.

Internet Research

Create a Flyer on an Incentive Program

Data Files

The owner of Terra Travel Services is offering an incentive to motivate travel consultants to increase travel bookings. The incentive is a sales contest with the grand prize of a one-week paid vacation to Cancun, Mexico. The owner has asked you to create a flyer that will be posted on the office bulletin board that includes information about the incentive program, as well as information about Cancun. Create this flyer using information about Cancun that you find on the Internet. Consider using one (or more) of the Cancun images (Cancun01.jpg, Cancun02.jpg, Cancun03.jpg, and Cancun04.jpg). Include any other information or objects to add visual interest to the flyer. Save the completed flyer and name it **U2-CancunFlyer**. Print and then close the document.

Job Study

Develop Recycling Program Communications

Data Files

The chief operating officer of Harrington Engineering has just approved your draft of the company's new recycling policy. (Open the file named **RecyclingPolicy.docx**) Edit the draft and prepare a final copy of the policy, along with a memo to all employees describing the new guidelines. To support the company's energy resources conservation effort, you will send hard copies of the new policy to the president of the Somerset Recycling Program and to the directors of the Somerset Chamber of Commerce.

Using the concepts and techniques you learned in this unit, prepare the following documents:

- Format the recycling policy manual, including a cover page, appropriate headers and footers, and page numbers. Add at least one graphic where appropriate. Format the document using styles and a style set. Save the manual and name it **U2-RecyclingManual**. Print the manual.
- Download a memo template at the New backstage area and then create a memo from Susan Gerhardt, Chief Operating Officer of Harrington Engineering, to all employees that introduces the new recycling program.